THE POETRY OF

MATTHEW PRIOR

Selected by
Hugh Parry

First published 2014
Hugh Parry asserts the moral right to be identified as the author of this book. The contents of this book are copyright © and may not be stored, copied or reproduced by any means without the written consent of the author.

CONTENTS

Foreword 1

The Scribbling Habit 3

Vanitas Vanitatum 11

Affairs of State 21

Cupid's Darts 28

A Natural Interlude 57

Asking the Big Questions 71

Let's Talk of Graves and Worms and Epitaphs 79

Index of Titles 82

FOREWORD

In his lifetime, Matthew Prior was considered to be one of the leading poets of the age. This esteem was achieved despite his amateur status as a literary man. He was also (primarily, as he would have said) a diplomat, a bureaucrat, a politician and a spy; a drafter of treaties and a negotiator for the Government at the highest level, often with a workload that prevented much dabbling in what he implied was just a versifying hobby. As is the way with hobbies, though, it was a need more than an indulgence. His output was quite considerable in the circumstances, partly because his reputation, which he seems to have cultivated rather than resented, conferred on him the status of an unofficial Poet Laureate to the Court and tacitly obliged him to produce occasional verse for a wide circle of friends.

Poetry of this kind, however, whatever favours it did him politically and socially in his own day, does him no favours now. A casually curious reader could dip into his work (assuming that the difficulty of finding a text had been overcome), chance to light upon a sycophantic ode or a cluster of trite erotic lyrics, and lose all will to proceed. Prior was appreciated by his contemporaries for technical gracefulness, but most of all for his entertainment value. The purpose of this booklet is to present his most appealing profile in order to prove that he can indeed still engage and amuse.

To this end, I have given some poems in their entirety, but have also felt free to select passages from poems which have interest but perhaps fail to 'travel' quite so well, and also from long works such as 'Alma' and 'Solomon' which nobody but the academic specialist would be likely to feel motivated to tackle, at least before swallowing the bait of a few appetising extracts.

My limited scope precludes a formal biography. An attempt at providing one would show an important aspect of the man and would involve the need to untangle and illuminate a long period of intricate political manoeuvring, but it would also show how little of his professional life was allowed to intrude into his poetry. In a fragmentary jotting, he noted that: 'Virtue and Love instruct me well / What to conceal and what to tell', but diplomacy taught him the same lesson.

The text used is that of the 1784 Edinburgh edition of the 3-volume 'Bell's Poets' of 1777, available in facsimile in the Elibron Classics series. An extraordinary feature of Prior's literary legacy is that a large number of poems only came to light at the beginning of the 20th century when papers of his were examined which had been stashed away in Longleat. I am therefore also using the Cambridge University Press text published in 1907, <u>Dialogues of the Dead and other works in prose and verse</u>, edited by A.R. Waller.

Prior's use of capitalisation in his manuscripts is inconsistent, so I have had no qualms about modernising the text in this regard, especially since Bell's edition had already done so in accordance with changing usage. Since my aim has been to stress Prior's delightful readability, I have seen no virtue in retaining archaic spellings, but my regularisation of past tenses to eliminate the copious apostrophes ('advanced' and 'varied' rather than 'advanc'd' and 'vary'd') is more contentious. I would argue that 18th century practice justifies itself only in so far as it enables the reader to distinguish between a voiced and a silent 'e', and Prior avoids the former (e.g. 'advancèd'); likewise, it seems pointless now to indicate elision in nominal two-syllable words such as 'heav'n' and 'pow'r' which the reader will naturally adjust to if necessary. Punctuation has been altered freely when it seemed that meaning could be clarified.

THE SCRIBBLING HABIT

A gentleman may cultivate the art of poetry as a worthy fruit from the stock of general refinement which is his family heritage, and on which has been grafted an education based on inculcating linguistic and literary skills; or poetry may be regarded as a pastime to fill all those empty leisure hours, rather less harmful than whist and mistresses. But Prior was a gentleman by a sustained act of will, and was able to say truthfully, if not very seriously, that he might even have plied a trade instead of being seduced into the composition of verses. His father was a joiner, who died when Matt was eleven, and his uncles were innkeepers: successful tradesmen, but with limited aspirations for the youngster:

> My uncle, rest his soul, when living,
> Might have contrived me ways of thriving,
> Taught me with cider to replenish
> My vats or ebbing tide of Rhenish.
> So when, for Hock, I drew pricked white wine, [sour]
> Swear 't had the flavour and was right wine; [proper]
> Or sent me with ten pounds to Furni-
> val's Inn to some good rogue attorney,
> Where now, by forging deeds and cheating,
> I'd found some handsome ways of getting.
>   All this you made me quit, to follow
> That sneaking, whey-faced god Apollo;
> Sent me among a fiddling crew
> Of folks I'd never seen nor knew,
> Calliope, and God knows who.   [Muse of epic poetry]
> To add no more invectives to it,
> You spoiled a youth to make a poet.
> ['An Epistle to Fleetwood Shephard Esq., 1689']

Not that he knew at this point how high-powered his career would be. This jocular accusation of misleading his impressionable immaturity is made to an older friend when Prior was only 25 and apparently headed for an academic life; already a young man of scholarly distinction, he could afford to be flippant about becoming a publican or vintner adulterating his goods or a pettifogging lawyer, but these were likely fates for somebody of his background, and it is remarkable with what facility he bypassed social obstacles, integrating smoothly with his natural charm and tact into the milieu of the aristocracy and intelligentsia.

Poetry was never going to be a viable way of life, and he tended to shrug off its importance:

> Repent, fond mortal, and be timely wise;
> Take heed, nor be by gilded hopes betrayed:
> Clio's a jilt, and Pegasus a jade.
> By verse you'll starve ...

(Clio was the Muse of history; to ride on Pegasus was to be poetically inspired.)

Ignore that warning, and be plagued with a life of disillusion, culminating in the traditional terminus of the unappreciated and the unemployed:

> When age and poverty comes faster on,
> And sad experience tells thou art undone,
> May no kind country grammar-school afford
> Ten pounds a year to pay for bed and board;
> Till, void of any fixed employ, and now
> Grown useless to the army and the plough,
> You've no friend left but trusting landlady,
> Who stows you on hard truckle, garret-high,
> To dream of dinner, and curse Poetry.
> ['A Satire upon the Poets']

Much later, in 1706, he dismissively remarked: 'it is long since I have (or at least ought to have) quitted Parnassus, and all the flowery roads on that side the country, though I thought myself indispensably obliged, upon the present occasion, to take a little journey into those parts.' This revisitation of old haunts was required in order to enable the writing of an Ode, supposedly in the style of Spenser, comprising a 350-line eulogy of Queen Anne and Marlborough that hardly took him beyond Parnassus Base Camp.

In fact, this was a routine gesture of self-deprecation, reinforced by a lingering awkwardness about the care he devoted to his pastime. The poetic virus cannot be eliminated, but self-control or the pressure of external events may modify the symptoms:

'As to poetry ... I would advise no man to attempt it except he cannot help it; and, if he cannot, it is in vain to dissuade him from it ... The greatest care imaginable must be taken of those who have this particular bent of thought: they must begin soon and continue long in the course of some severer studies. As to

my own part, I found this impulse very soon, and shall continue to feel it as long as I can think; I remember nothing further in life than that I made verses. I chose Guy of Warwick for my first hero and killed Colborn the Giant before I was big enough for Westminster School. But I had two accidents in youth which hindered me from being quite possessed with the Muse: I was bred in a College where prose was more in fashion than verse, and as soon as I had taken my first degree was sent the King's Secretary to The Hague. There I had enough to do in studying French and Dutch and altering my Terentian and Virgilian style into that of Articles, Conventions and Memorials, so that poetry, which by the bent of my mind might have become the business of my life, was, by the happiness of my education, only the amusement of it ...'
['An Essay upon Learning'; Guy of Warwick was the protagonist of one of the most popular Medieval romances; three years separated his degree and the post in Holland, so his chronology is disingenuous.]

The churning out of bureaucratic prose may have saved him from poetic scribbling, but, when he *was* versifying, he blamed it for his inability to write in an exalted vein:

> But we must change the style – Just now I said
> I ne'er was master of the tuneful trade;
> Or the small genius which my youth could boast,
> In prose and business lies extinct and lost ...
> ['A Letter to Monsieur Boileau Despreaux']

How is a simple Muse to follow King William into the rarefied stratosphere of heroic achievement?:

> Till, lost in trackless fields of shining day,
> Unable to discern the way,
> Which Nassau's virtue only could explore,
> Untouched, unknown to any Muse before,
> She, from the noble precipices thrown,
> Comes rushing with uncommon ruin down.
> Glorious attempt! unhappy fate!
> The song too daring and the theme too great!
> ['Carmen Seculare', 301-8]

In one of his 'Dialogues of the Dead', he quotes himself, through the mouth of the Emperor Charles, and comments on this wryly but honestly in the person of the grammarian who is puncturing the monarch's self-importance: 'Prior may say what he will in verse: that Hymn was all Enthusiasm; all Heroes – Stars and Gods. In prose, I am sure he is of another opinion.' ['Charles and Clenard']

This surely constitutes a word of warning never to forget the pinch of salt as an accompaniment to Prior's poetic mode.

The modest disclaimers of ability could simultaneously invite the reassuring response that he had no cause to question his talent and yet subtly hint that he knew his manner in those quasi-laureate odes was inflated. After all, his signature tune was the vanity of human wishes. The ecstatic admiration he professed for William's martial prowess must be set against this melancholy aria on the transience of glory, conventional in sentiment and indebted to Juvenal, but no less fine for that:

> What is a king? A man condemned to bear
> The public burden of the nation's care;
> Now crowned, some angry faction to appease,
> Now falls a victim to the people's ease;
> From the first blooming of his ill-taught youth,
> Nourished in flattery and estranged from truth;
> At home, surrounded by a servile crowd,
> Prompt to abuse, and in detraction loud;
> Abroad, begirt with men and swords and spears,
> His very state acknowledging his fears;
> Marching amidst a thousand guards, he shows
> His secret terror of a thousand foes;
> In war, however prudent, great or brave,
> To blind events and fickle chance a slave;
> Seeking to settle what for ever flies,
> Sure of the toil, uncertain of the prize.
>   But he returns with conquest on his brow,
> Brings up the triumph and absolves the vow:
> The captive generals to his car are tied;
> The joyful citizens' tumultuous tide,
> Echoing his glory, gratify his pride.
> What is this triumph? Madness, shouts and noise,
> One great collection of the people's voice.
> The wretches he brings back in chains relate
> What may tomorrow be the victor's fate;
> The spoils and trophies borne before him show
> National loss and epidemic woe,
> Various distress which he and his may know.
> Does he not mourn the valiant thousands slain,
> The heroes, once the glory of the plain,

> Left in the conflict of the fatal day,
> Or the wolf's portion, or the vulture's prey?
> Does he not weep the laurel which he wears,
> Wet with the soldiers' blood and widows' tears?
>   See where he comes, the darling of the war!
> See millions crowding round the gilded car!
> In the vast joys of this ecstatic hour,
> And full fruition of successful power,
> One moment and one thought might let him scan
> The various turns of life and fickle state of man.
> Are the dire images of sad distrust
> And popular change obscured amid the dust
> That rises from the victor's rapid wheel?
> Can the loud clarion or the shrill fife repel
> The inward cries of Care? Can Nature's voice,
> Plaintive, be drowned or lessened in the noise,
> Though shouts as thunder loud afflict the air,
> Stun the birds (now released), and shake the ivory
>   chair?
> ['Solomon' III/275-322]

Or you may prefer this laconic but resonant epigram:

> Blest be the princes who have fought
> For pompous names or wide dominion,
> Since by their error we are taught
> That happiness is but opinion.

This may be read as suggesting that public esteem ('opinion') is the yardstick by which ambitious princes measure their happiness (a word that shades into the sense of 'good fortune'); but 'error' more logically implies a mistaken belief (their *own* opinion) in the satisfaction to be gained from setting and achieving grandiose goals.

Even sceptical poets are of course keen to promote verse as the most effective preservative of greatness, so William was urged to resuscitate 'the drooping Muses' because:

> To them by smiling Jove 'twas given to save
> Distinguished patriots from the common grave;
> To them great William's glory to recall,
> When statues moulder and when arches fall.
> ['Carmen Seculare', 456-9]

However, the vanity of majesty and conquest was exposed in 'Solomon' only after a glum refutation of the comforting belief in the power of artistic achievement to cheat mortality, with some more mouldering to deplore:

> Your very fear of death shall make you try
> To catch the shade of immortality,
> Wishing on earth to linger, and to save
> Part of its prey from the devouring grave;
> To those who may survive ye to bequeath
> Something entire in spite of time and death;
> A fancied kind of being to retrieve,
> And in a book, or from a building, live.
> False hope! Vain labour! Let some ages fly,
> The dome shall moulder and the volume die.
> ['Solomon', III, 257-66]

Not that poets deserve much credit even if their works do for a short while outlive them, because the theory of inspiration, if viewed from a cynical angle, turns the creative process into ventriloquism:

> Here some would scratch their heads, and try
> What they should write, and how, and why;
> But I conceive such folk are quite in
> Mistakes in theory of writing.
> If once for principle 'tis laid
> That thought is trouble to the head,
> I argue thus: the world agrees
> That he writes well who writes with ease;
> Then he, by sequel logical,
> Writes best who never thinks at all.
>   Verse comes from heaven like inward light;
> Mere human pains can ne'er come by 't;
> The god, not we, the poem makes;
> We only tell folks what he speaks.
> Hence, when anatomists discourse
> How like brutes' organs are to ours,
> They grant, if higher powers think fit,
> A bear might soon be made a wit,
> And that, for anything in Nature,
> Pigs might squeak love-odes, dogs bark satire.

The literal meaning of ventriloquism, speaking from the stomach, is ingloriously coupled in the same poem with Prior's version of monkeys with typewriters eventually composing Shakespeare:

> ... when you poets swear and cry,
> "The god inspires, I rave, I die!";
> If inward wind does truly swell ye,
> It must be the colic in your belly:
> That writing is but just like dice,
> And lucky mains make people wise: [throws]
> That jumbled words, if Fortune throw 'em,
> Shall well as Dryden form a poem,
> Or make a speech correct and witty,
> As you know who – at the committee.

('An Epistle to Fleetwood Shephard Esq.', May 1689; the reference to Dryden is *intended* to be rude – Prior co-wrote a scathing satire on Dryden's apologia for Roman Catholicism, 'The Hind and the Panther'.)

This denigration of poetic creativity is obviously playful, but Prior knew his tendency to use verse as an excuse to indulge his most whimsical notions. He has been expounding his theories about the soul to his friend with fanciful zeal for a thousand lines until the victim protests:

> Richard, who now was half asleep,
> Roused, nor would longer silence keep ...
> "As folks", quoth Richard, "prone to leasing   [lying]
> Say things at first because they're pleasing,
> Then prove what they have once asserted,
> Nor care to have their lie deserted,
> Till their own dreams at length deceive 'em,
> And, oft repeating, they believe 'em;
> Or as, again, those amorous blades
> Who trifle with their mothers' maids,
> Though at the first their wild desire
> Was but to quench a present fire,
> Yet if the object of their love
> Chance by Lucina's aid to prove,

[Lucina is the goddess of childbirth; 'prove' to be with child, and also swell or rise in pregnancy, like dough]

> They seldom let the bantling roar   [brat]
> In basket at a neighbour's door,
> But, by the flattering glass of Nature
> Viewing themselves in Cakebread's feature,

>   With serious thought and care support
>   What only was begun in sport.
>   Just so with you, my friend, it fares,
>   Who deal in philosophic wares:
>   Atoms you cut, and forms you measure,
>   To gratify your private pleasure,
>   Till airy deeds of casual wit
>   Do some fantastic birth beget;
>   And, pleased to find your system mended
>   Beyond what you at first intended,
>   The happy whimsey you pursue
>   Till you at length believe it true:
>   Caught by your own delusive art,
>   You fancy first, and then assert."
>   ['Alma', III/1-2, 9-38]

There is some truth there, but Prior takes the sting out of it by the image of the illegitimate child, which is not only comical but of deliberately dubious relevance, since seducers of maids do not invariably succumb to a surge of paternal pride. Anyway, those who cannot enjoy whimsey should abandon Prior and switch, perhaps, to Milton – was it Prior or his co-author who said: 'I hate such a rough unhewn fellow as Milton, that a man must sweat to read him.' The speaker is a complacent poetaster proud of his own smooth style: 'Egad, you may run over this and be almost asleep.' ['The Hind and the Panther Transversed']

That was not intended as an expression of Prior's personal taste, but it is surprising to see how ineptly he handled blank verse on the one occasion when he seriously attempted it; no wonder he left the poem unfinished, although he observed of his own practice that 'he that writes in rhymes dances in fetters'.

VANITAS VANITATUM

Prior's conviction of the vanity of human wishes underlies every aspect of life on which he touches, not just the folly of believing that poetry can confer immortality on either the subject or the author:

> Happiness! object of that waking dream
> Which we call Life, mistaking; fugitive theme
> Of my pursuing verse; ideal shade,
> Notional good; by fancy only made,
> And by tradition nursed; fallacious fire,
> Whose dancing beams mislead our fond desire;
> Cause of our care, and error of our mind;
> Oh! hadst thou ever been by Heaven designed
> To Adam and his mortal race, the boon
> Entire had been reserved for Solomon;
> On me the partial lot had been bestowed,
> And in my cup the golden draught had flowed.
>   But O! ere yet original man was made,
> Ere the foundations of this earth were laid,
> It was opponent to our search ordained:
> That joy, still sought, should never be attained ...
> ['Solomon', I/14-29]

'Solomon' is Prior's most determined effort to elevate his themes and transcend the light verse and the panegyrics which he was associated with. Solomon's attempt to fulfil himself by means of illusions such as the pursuit of knowledge or love, unavailing despite the possession of almost unmatchable advantages to smooth his path, is likely to leave a reader more exasperated than sympathetic, although there are fine poetic set-pieces along the way. It doesn't help that the lines quoted above define at the very beginning of the poem the hopelessness of a quest which we are asked to take an interest in for a further two and a half thousand lines. Do we want to follow doggedly to his logical conclusion that the dead are lucky, that those who live for the shortest time are luckier, but that luckiest of all are those who never emerge into the whole farrago of existence?

> But O! beyond description happiest he
> Who ne'er must roll on life's tumultuous sea;
> Who, with blest freedom from the general doom
> Exempt, must never force the teeming womb,
> Nor see the sun, nor sink into the tomb.   [III/235-9]

This pointless reductio ad absurdum is a product of the adoption of a melancholy which is occasionally indulged as a pose. The essence of his philosophy is cynical enough, but the true Prior saw Folly as an almost indomitable guide and ally – mercifully for us:

> TO THE HONOURABLE CHARLES MONTAGUE, ESQ.
>
> I
>
> Howe'er, 'tis well that, while mankind
> Through Fate's perverse meander errs,
> He can imagined pleasures find
> To combat against real cares.
>
> II
>
> Fancies and notions he pursues
> Which ne'er had being but in thought;
> Each, like the Grecian artist, woos   [Pygmalion]
> The image he himself has wrought.
>
> III
>
> Against experience he believes;
> He argues against demonstration;
> Pleased when his reason he deceives,
> And sets his judgment by his passion.
>
> IV
>
> The hoary fool, who many days
> Has struggled with continued sorrow,
> Renews his hope, and blindly lays
> The desperate bet upon tomorrow.
>
> V
>
> Tomorrow comes; 'tis noon, 'tis night:
> This day like all the former flies;
> Yet on he runs to seek delight
> Tomorrow, till tonight he dies.
>
> VI
>
> Our hopes like towering falcons aim

At objects in an airy height:
The little pleasure of the game
Is from afar to view the flight.

VII

Our anxious pains we all the day
In search of what we like employ;
Scorning at night the worthless prey,
We find the labour gave the joy.

VIII

At distance through an artful glass,
To the mind's eye things well appear;
They lose their forms, and make a mass
Confused and black, if brought too near.

IX

If we see right, we see our woes:
Then what avails it to have eyes?
From ignorance our comfort flows:
The only wretched are the wise.

X

We wearied should lie down in death:
This cheat of life would take [appeal] no more
If you thought fame but an empty breath,
I Phyllis but a perjured whore.

Building castles in the air and houses upon sand is such a serious game that it becomes for most of us the business of life. The game must be played with relish and determination, futile as it may be, since the caperings of folly are all that can divert us as we face the inconveniences of our stubborn will to live:

> The man in graver tragic known   [i.e. tragedy]
> (Though his best part long since was done)
> Still on the stage desires to tarry,
> And he who played the Harlequin
> After the jest still loads the scene,
> Unwilling to retire, though weary.
> ['Written in the beginning of Mezeray's History of France']

Prior's wry amusement at the figures we cut can be illustrated by the treatment of his own weakness for collecting. His elegant London house was stuffed with objets d'art, yet, as we have seen, he knew that the problem with false or exaggerated values is that acquisition is everything and completion is fatal:

> What toil did honest Curio take,
> What strict enquiries did he make,
> To get one medal, wanting yet,
> And perfect all his Roman set?
> 'Tis found: and, O, his happy lot!
> 'Tis bought, locked up, and lies forgot:
> Of these no more you hear him speak;
> He now begins upon the Greek.
> These, ranged and showed, shall in their turns
> Remain obscure as in their urns.   [unseen]
> ['Alma', III/448-57]

Why collect medals (as Prior himself did)? Well, they are educational:

'Medals are, again, a help to chronology, but the scarcity and expense of good ones make it difficult for any man less than a Prince to possess such a series of them as shall be of real use to him. For here I make the greatest difference imaginable between study and curiosity, since one is to profit the mind, the t'other to please the eye. The gentleman who likes medals very well will always be desirous to possess the best of them, and the antiquary or vertuose will be sure to top false ones upon him, besides that too much money may be spent in the acquisition, too much time may be spent in the contemplation of them.'
['An Essay upon Learning']

Our hankering above all for rarities is mocked in another essay, 'Upon Opinion':

'The various estimate we make as to the value of things cannot be better illustrated than by the wants we find in the pursuit of our studies, every man adding to his heap, and desirous to complete his collection: books, pictures, medals, nay, dried flowers, insects, cockleshells – anything will do; but then, the cruel losses which we sometimes sustain – the late Monarch and Court of France were all disturbed, and Charles Patin was banished the kingdom, because it was suspected by some that the Otho which he sold the King was not genuine [a Roman coin or medal]; perhaps a little boy yesterday at Canterbury tore that butterfly in pieces, or at Dover threw the very shell into the sea, the species of which were the only ones now missing in Sir Hans Sloan's cabinet, and an oilman on Fish Street Hill did actually wrap up his anchovies in the first Horace that was ever printed ...

Prior winced as he thought of his cherished accumulations being treated as just so much lumber after his death by distant relations utterly unaware of their value to the cognoscenti and flogging his treasures by the weight:

> Those who could never read their grammar,
> When my dear volumes touch the hammer,
> May think books best as richest bound;
> My copper medals by the pound
> May be with learnèd justice weighed;
> To turn the balance, Otho's head
> May be thrown in; and for the metal
> The coin may mend a tinker's kettle ...
> ['Alma', III/570-7]

He addresses Alma, the human soul, with derision for its ability to be infinitely diverted with trumpery:

> Now, Alma, to divines and prose
> I leave thy frauds and crimes and woes,
> Nor think tonight of thy ill-nature
> But of thy follies, idle creature,
> The turns of thy uncertain wing,
> And not the malice of thy sting.
> Thy pride of being great and wise
> I do but mention to despise;
> I view with anger and disdain
> How little gives thee joy or pain:
> A print, a bronze, a flower, a root,
> A shell, a butterfly can do't:
> Even a romance, a tune, a rhyme
> Help thee to pass the tedious time,
> Which else would on thy hand remain –
> Though, flown, it ne'er looks back again;
> And cards are dealt, and chessboards brought,
> To ease the pain of coward thought.
> Happy result of human wit!
> That Alma may herself forget.

['Alma', III/472-91]

We know that, even as he writes this, he is thinking of that one particular coin which at the moment is nothing but a maddeningly empty space in his curio cabinet – and he knows we know.

The following poem may seem to have no connection with the pricking of collectors' mania, but its relevance will eventually emerge. In the meantime, it is perhaps a welcome lightening of the mood. It is apparently all set to be a re-telling of Ovid's account in <u>Metamorphoses</u> of Baucis and Philemon, the old couple who offer hospitality to Jupiter and Mercury after their richer neighbours have all kept their doors shut. The gods in retaliation flood the whole area, but transform the cottage of their hosts into a temple and undertake to grant any boon which they crave. After a quick consultation, the couple ask to be the priests in the new temple and that both should die in the same hour. There is another traditional motif flowing into this story, though: the offer by a grateful or kindly fairy to fulfil three wishes, which the recipients misuse (a sinister variant on this is the well-known story, 'The Monkey's Paw').

THE LADLE

The Sceptics think 'twas long ago
Since gods came down incognito
To see who were their friends or foes,
And how our actions fell or rose;
That, since they gave things their beginning
And set this whirligig a-spinning,
Supine they in their heaven remain,
Exempt from passion and from pain,
And frankly leave us human elves
To cut and shuffle for ourselves:
To stand or walk, to rise or tumble,
As matter and as motion jumble.
  The poets, now, and painters hold
This thesis both absurd and bold,
And your good-natured gods, they say,
Descend some twice or thrice a day,
Else all these things we toil so hard in
Would not avail one single farthing;
For when the hero we rehearse   [Aeneas, here]
To grace his actions and our verse,
'Tis not by dint of human thought
That to his Latium he is brought:

Iris descends by Fate's commands
  To guide his steps through foreign lands,
  And Amphitrite clears his way   [a sea-nymph]
  From rocks and quicksands in the sea.
    And if you see him in a sketch
  (Though drawn by Paulo or Carache),
[Agostino Carracci and, probably, Paolo Farinati – Italian artists and print-makers of the 16th century]
  He shows not half his force and strength
  Strutting in armour and at length:
  That he may make his proper figure,
  The piece must yet be four yards bigger:
  The nymphs conduct him to the field –
  One holds his sword and one his shield –
  Mars, standing by, asserts his quarrel,
  And Fame flies after with a laurel.
    These points, I say, of speculation
  (As 'twere to save or sink the nation),
  Men idly learnèd will dispute,
  Assert, object, confirm, refute;
  Each mighty angry, mighty right,
  With equal arms sustains the fight,
  Till now no umpire can agree 'em,
  So both draw off and sing Te Deum.
    Is it in equilibrio
  If deities descend or no?
  Then let the affirmative prevail,
  As requisite to form my tale,
  For by all parties 'tis confessed
  That those opinions are the best
  Which in their nature most conduce
  To present ends and private use.
    Two gods came, therefore, from above:
  One, Mercury – the other, Jove.
  The humour was, it seems, to know
  If all the favours they bestow
  Could from our own perverseness ease us,
  And if our wish, enjoyed, would please us.
  Discoursing largely on this theme,
  O'er hills and dales their godships came,
  Till, well-nigh tired at almost night,
  They thought it proper to alight.
    Note here, that it as true as odd is,
  That in disguise a god or goddess
  Exerts no supernatural powers,
  But acts on maxims much like ours.

They spied at last a country farm,
Where all was snug and clean and warm;
For woods before and hills behind
Secured it both from rain and wind;
Large oxen in the field were lowing,
Good grain was sowed, good fruit was growing;
Of last year's corn in barns great store;
Fat turkeys gobbling at the door;
And Wealth, in short, with Peace consented
That people here should live contented.
But did they in effect do so?
Have patience, friend, and thou shalt know.
   The honest farmer and his wife,
To years declined from prime of life,
Had struggled with the marriage noose,
As almost every couple does:
Sometimes "My plague!", sometimes "My darling!",
Kissing today, tomorrow snarling;
Jointly submitting to endure
That evil which admits no cure.
   Our gods the outward gate unbarred;
Our farmer met 'em in the yard,
Thought they were folks that lost their way,
And asked them civilly to stay;
Told 'em, for supper or for bed
They might go on and be worse sped.
   So said, so done; the gods consent;
All three into the parlour went;
They compliment, they sit, they chat,
Fight o'er the wars, reform the state;
A thousand knotty points they clear,
Till supper and my wife appear.
   Jove made his leg and kissed the dame;
Obsequious Hermes did the same.
"Jove kissed the farmer's wife!", you say.
He did – but in an honest way;
Oh! not with half that warmth and life
With which he kissed Amphitryon's wife.
[Hercules was the result of this union]
   Well then, things handsomely were served:
My mistress for the strangers carved.
How strong the beer, how good the meat,
How loud they laughed, how much they eat,
In epic sumptuous would appear,
Yet shall be passed in silence here:
For I should grieve to have it said

That, by a fine description led,
I made my episode too long
Or tired my friend to grace my song.
  The grace-cup served, the cloth away,
Jove thought it time to show his play.
"Landlord and landlady", he cried,
"Folly and jesting laid aside,
That ye thus hospitably live,
And strangers with good cheer receive,
Is mighty grateful to your betters,
And makes e'en gods themselves your debtors.
To give this thesis plainer proof,
You have tonight beneath your roof
A pair of gods – nay, never wonder –
This youth can fly and I can thunder.
I'm Jupiter, and he Mercurius –
My page, my son (indeed, but spurious).
Form then three wishes, you and Madam,
And, sure as you already had 'em,
The things desired, in half an hour,
Shall all be here and in your power."
  "Thank ye, great gods!", the woman says;
"Oh! may your altars ever blaze!
A Ladle for our silver dish
Is what I want, is what I wish."
"A Ladle!", cries the man, "A Ladle!
Odzooks, Corisca, you have prayed ill!
What should be great you turn to farce –
I wish the Ladle in your a---."
  With equal grief and shame my Muse
The sequel of the tale pursues.
The Ladle fell into the room,
And stuck in old Corisca's bum.
Our couple weep two wishes past,
And kindly join to form the last:
To ease the woman's awkward pain,
And get the Ladle out again.

MORAL

This commoner has worth and parts,
Is praised for arms or loved for arts;
His head aches for a coronet,
And who is blest that is not great?
  Some sense and more estate kind Heaven
To this well-lotted peer has given;

What then? He must have rule and sway,
And all is wrong till he's in play.   [gambling]
The miser must make up his plum,
And dares not touch the hoarded sum;
The sickly dotard wants a wife
To draw off his last dregs of life.
   Against our peace we arm our will:
Amidst our plenty, something still
For horses, houses, pictures, planting,
To thee, to me, to him is wanting:
That cruel something unpossessed
Corrodes and leavens all the rest;
That something if we could obtain
Would soon create a future pain;
And to the coffin from the cradle,
'Tis all a wish and all a Ladle.

The narrative, as well as having a comically discursive introduction (which testifies to Prior's interest in art), displays the boisterousness and the gleeful bad taste of the medieval fabliau, best known in English through Chaucer's tales of the Miller and the Reeve. The moral, however, can now be seen as pure Prior.

AFFAIRS OF STATE

Could Prior's view on vanity fail to affect his observations on politics? He had to watch his step, of course: avoid satire, he dryly warned a young would-be writer, if you want a thriving career. It is tricky to assess his eulogies because they are so alien to the temper of a pseudo-egalitarian modern democracy which is characterised by cynicism towards authority. Prior discoursed eloquently on the vicissitudes and burdens that make a position of power almost intolerable. Also, as a witty, gregarious, erudite and articulate man, he must have been perfectly aware of William III's charmlessness; furthermore, he could not have failed to see Queen Anne's mediocrity, and would have known that she was snobbishly averse to advancing the career of a base-born upstart whose first job was helping in a pub. So is this sort of thing sheer sycophantic gush?:

> Namur, proud city, how her towers were armed!
> How she contemned the approaching foe!
> Till she by William's trumpets was alarmed,
> And shook and sunk and fell beneath his blow.
> Jove and Pallas, mighty powers,
> Guided the hero to the hostile towers.
> Perseus seemed less swift in war
> When, winged with speed, he flew through air.
> Embattled nations strive in vain
> The hero's glory to restrain;
> Streams armed with rocks, and mountains red with fire
> In vain against his force conspire.
> Behold him from the dreadful height appear!
> And lo! Britannia's Lions waving there.
> ['Carmen Seculare', 173-86]

What about this ardent plea for a portrait?:

> Will thy indulgent hand, fair Saint, allow
> The boon? And will thy ear accept the vow?
> That in despite of age, of impious flame,
> And eating Time, thy picture, like thy fame,
> Entire may last: that, as their eyes survey
> The semblant shade, men yet unborn may say,
> "Thus great, thus gracious looked Britannia's Queen,
> Her brow thus smooth, her look was thus serene ..."
> ['An Epistle. Desiring the Queen's Picture']

Prior never finished this second poem because he learned, in the middle of his rapturous composition, that the Queen had died, which removed the point of the request. On to the next, then:

> Illustrious George now fills the throne,
> Our wise, benign, good king;
> Who can his wondrous deeds make known,
> Or his bright actions sing?
> ['The Viceroy']

His heart wasn't in this doggerel, and the 'bright action' which this ballad highlighted was the King's promotion of Lord Coningsby, whose earlier corrupt depradations as the Irish Viceroy were attacked with an uncharacteristic savagery worthy of Swift.

It is all but impossible to accept that Prior wrote these encomia with completely genuine personal enthusiasm for the royals whom he was apotheosising. But when he came to publish his poems, his 'Public Panegyrics' formed one of the four categories into which he divided his work (the others were 'Amorous Odes', 'Idle Tales' and 'Serious Reflections'), so there was no question of shame-faced expurgation, no muttering about their being a necessary response to the exigencies of the time. It must be assumed that he thought they were good, or at least that they would be appreciated by his readers.

What is beyond doubt is his patriotism. Even Solomon is vouchsafed a vision of Britannia to look forward to as compensation for the dismal prophesies of the disasters awaiting Israel. More significant than whether he really believed that William outranked every hero of classical antiquity is whether the King for him represented a bastion of Protestantism; Churchill asserted that 'As a sovereign and commander he was entirely without religious prejudices ... He used religious questions as counters in his political combinations' (A History of the English-speaking Peoples). Never mind whether Anne and Marlborough were comparable to Jove and his eagle – was the British army in her reign and under his command repelling Louis XIV's megalomanic encroachments?

A more difficult question is: to what extent did Prior seriously think that the English Government was on a crusade to emancipate the world from tyranny, requiring him to volunteer as a stop-gap local Virgil?:

> Arms and a Queen to sing, who, great and good,
> From peaceful Thames to Danube's wondering flood,
> Sent forth the terror of her high commands
> To save the nations from invading hands,
> To prop fair Liberty's declining cause,
> And fix the jarring world with equal laws.
> ['A Letter to Monsieur Boileau Despreaux', 1704]

One may look askance at his assertion that Britain's foes were rather pleased to be defeated because they were always treated with such magnanimity, but Louis's France was a convenient yardstick against which to measure personal liberties and constitutional equilibrium as far as these ideas went in the early 18th century. When he sneeringly debunked Boileau verse by verse for the almost blasphemous adulation of his monarch, we may find Prior's hypocrisy breathtaking, but he would no doubt have refused to accept that this was a case of pots and kettles. What's wrong with agit-prop if it's *right*?

On the other hand, there is the shadowy Prior who, like any diplomat, adopted the line of 'My Country, Right or Wrong', knowing that he would have to take up negotiating positions which he abhorred; privately, he dropped a hint or two about this which was never allowed to sully the stream of his patriotic verse. But one little squib lurking amongst his manuscripts does detonate questions that crack the façade somewhat:

> A FABLE
>
> In Aesop's Tales an honest wretch we find,
> Whose years and comforts equally declined;
> He in two wives had two domestic ills,
> For different age they had, and different wills:
> One plucked his black hairs out, and one his grey.
> The man for quietness did both obey,
> Till all his parish saw his head quite bare,
> And thought he wanted brains as well as hair.

That may not seem at all explosive – trivial and chauvinistic, no doubt. Then comes the interpretation:

> THE MORAL
>
> The Parties, hen-pecked W----m, are thy wives,
> The hairs they pluck are thy prerogatives;
> Tories thy person hate, the Whigs thy power;

> Though much thou yieldest, still they tug for more,
> Till this poor man and thou alike are shown:
> He without hair, and thou without a crown.

The descent from William the superhero to William the henpecked husband is startling, and there can hardly be any doubt that Prior, letting off steam in a private lampoon, is expressing his true feelings here – indeed, the poem explains why he chose to alienate old friends by 'crossing the floor' and transferring his allegiance, not perhaps with ardency, to the Tories, who opposed the weakening of the monarchy which was caused by too many checks being imposed on its prerogatives. To those who regarded this as a betrayal, he would say: 'certain it is that the same man at different times alters his opinion of the same things.' However, his quizzical temperament would never be perfectly comfortable in any ideological confederation:

'A Party Man, indeed (and such most of us are, or must be), is an animal that no commentator upon human nature can sufficiently explain. He has not his opinion, how sorry a world soever it may be, in his own keeping. *Quo ad hoc* he is mad: must speak without believing what he understands; without enquiring, he acts as implicitly according to the word of command given out by the heads of his faction, as a Carthusian or a Jesuit does to the will of his Superior. The Lie of the Day is the rule of his life, and as his judgment depends upon that of other men, he must justify everything that his Party acts with the greatest injustice, till from the degrees of warm and violent he comes up to furious and wicked.'
['An Essay upon Opinion']

Party politics in fact nearly destroyed him. The Whig administration after Anne's death arrested him as part of their campaign to indict the Tories of treasonable offences in connection with the Treaty of Utrecht, signed in 1713, which ended the War of the Spanish Succession. Prior had played a key role in the negotiations and the drafting of the documents. He was held under house arrest, and his diplomatic career was over. Some of the bitterness and tension of this dangerous period seems to be anticipated in a few lines of 'Solomon':

> The judge corrupt, the long-depending cause
> [i.e. the protracted threat hanging over the victim]
> And doubtful issue of misconstrued laws;
> The crafty turns of a dishonest state
> And violent will of the wrong-doing great;

> The venomed tongue injurious to his fame,
> Which nor can wisdom shun nor fair advice reclaim.
> [III/202-7]

In retirement at his country seat, many years after being freed, he evoked a nightmarish legal persecution:

> For when your Judge becomes your foe,
> Think nor to give nor ward the blow;
> The danger prudently to shun,
> Forbear to plead and learn to run.
> What good can culprits, staying, do
> When laws explained by power pursue?
> Avails it aught what you can say,
> If all the Bench resolves the nay?
> When Truth outvoted comes too late,
> What does she but prevaricate?
> The circumstances change the case:
> 'Tis now no trial, but a race.
> What signifies Achilles' speed
> But to be rid in time of need?
> When angry Paris aimed the dart
> Against the hero's mortal part,
> Instead of fighting, had he fled,
> His heel might have secured his head.
> ['Fragments written at Down-Hall']

Then there is Prior identifying himself with St Sebastian:

> Who e'er a serious view will take
> Of that learn'd book the Almanack
> Will find a figur'd Man Pierc'd thrô
> With sundry Darts from head to toe
> Just so at least a Year stood I
> Smote breast and back and hip and Thigh
> Full twenty Foes around me came
> And each at me took several Aim
> Against some part each took
> One at my head with malice Stroke
> T'other ram'd Perjury at my throat
> This with Sophisticated reason
> [specious, convoluted]
> Shot at my hand for writing Treason
> Against Them All I stood.

(For once, I have reproduced the manuscript text unedited; its rough, unpunctuated state chillingly conveys an urgent, hysterical edge, so unlike the urbane Prior known to outsiders.)

He lost his entrée to the courts of Europe and a job which made particularly appropriate use of his linguistic talents; he was evidently upset by the backstabbing and the accusations of treachery. But he emerged with his neck intact, and such a sociable and intellectually curious man would be able to take to retirement better than many – with poetry to write, edit and publish as well.

Opinions of the same things change, as he said. Before we leave politics, let us look at a striking illustration of this. As a young man, he prepared an early bid for public notice by concocting a coronation ode, although it exists only in manuscript. He was already airing one of his favourite tropes, comparing the British monarch to inferior VIPs of old:

> Thus methinks I see the barge
> Pleased with the sacred weight of its majestic charge;
> Old Argo with a weight less glorious fraught
> The treasure from impoverished Colchos brought,
> And Hellespont, now vanquished, must confess
> His burthen meaner and his triumph less,

[this identifies the King as a latterday Xerxes, crossed with Leander]

> Since richer Thames does James and Mary bear:
> He great as Jove, she as Europa fair.
> They come! Joy doubles strength to every oar,
> Resounding echoes fill the crowded shore,
> The waves with an unusual pride
> Pay homage to the Lord
> Of our asserted Main,
> And calmly as they glide,
> Auspiciously afford
> An omen of his reign ...
>
> Triumphant Caesar in less glory rode
> When heightened from a Victor to a God ...
>   ['On the Coronation']

The living legend is James II, and Prior is a smart, ambitious young man, not quite 21, splashing him with hyperbolical admiration.

Another opportunity occurred in the same year. The Monmouth rebellion challenged the new monarch but collapsed rapidly, and the Duke was executed. Prior saw the whole thrilling drama as the ideal subject for a series of vivid tableaux; he liked to design paintings and sculptures in his head, claiming to envy painters for their access to a universal appreciation denied to writers restricted by the language they were using. The youngster's judgments are harsh: 'the misled, aspiring, wretched man, / His sword maintaining what his fraud began.' This is strongly-felt or diplomatic or both. But hints of ambivalence creep in as Monmouth's doom approaches:

> Now, artist, let thy juster pencil draw
> The sad effects of necessary law.
> In painted words and speaking colours, tell
> The dismal exit this sham Prince befell;
> On the sad scene the glorious rebel place,
> With pride and sorrow struggling in his face;
> Describe the pangs of his distracted breast
> (If by thy labours thought can be expressed);
> Show with what difference two vast passions move,
> And how the Hero with the Christian strove.
> ['Advice to the Painter, Upon the Defeat of the Rebels']

The upheaval looked altogether different from a later perspective, when there was nothing to be gained from supporting the discredited cause of the Stuarts. The rebellion was then adduced, in the 'Essay upon Opinion', as a supportive illustration of Prior's increasing scepticism:

'... as to Opinion, success qualifies the action ... We need not go from our own country or our own memory for instances of this kind: the Duke of Monmouth came to England with Liberty and Property and the Protestant Religion on his standard; he was beaten and beheaded; his honours were taken from his family. The Prince of Orange does the same thing: he is successful, is crowned King of England, transmits an immortal memory to posterity; gives us a new Epoch of Time, and a different set of principles from the Revolution.

Historical judgments are founded on respect for the winners in the lottery of Fate. ''Tis but fortune, all is fortune'.

CUPID'S DARTS

'The Corridors of Power' is a lazy cliché now. Novels, films, TV series, painstaking modern biographies and warts-and-all political diaries make us think we have walked down them in imagination, although undoubtedly 'we don't know the half of it'. Prior never offered himself as a guide in his poetry. We have one vignette of the working civil servant – and he's off-duty:

>THE SECRETARY. Written at The Hague 1696
>
>While with labour assiduous due pleasure I mix,
>And in one day atone for the business of six,
>In a little Dutch chaise, on a Saturday night,
>On my left hand my Horace, a w---- on my right;
>No memoirs [memos] to compose and no postboy to move,
>That on Sunday may hinder the softness of love;
>For her, neither visits nor parties at tea,
>Nor the long-winded cant of a dull refugee;
>This night and the next shall be hers, shall be mine –
>To good or ill fortune the third we resign.
>Thus, scorning the world, and superior to Fate,
>I drive on my car in processional state;
>So with Phia through Athens Pisistratus rode:
>Men thought her Minerva, and him a new god.
>[6th century ruler of Athens, known for moderation, but also political astuteness]
>But why should I stories of Athens rehearse,
>Where people knew love and were partial to verse,
>Since none can with justice my pleasure oppose
>In Holland, half drowned in interest and prose?
>['interest' is 'factionalism', but perhaps with subsidiary meaning of 'usury, profit-making']
>By Greece and past ages what need I be tried,
>When The Hague and the present are both on my side?
>And is it enough for the joys of the day
>To think what Anacreon or Sappho would say,
>[they would recommend drink and love respectively]
>When good Vandergoes and his provident Vrouw,
>As they gaze on my triumph, do freely allow
>That, search all the Province, you'll find no man dar is
>So blest as the *Englischen Heer Secretar* is.

The anapaestic rhythms mimic the jaunty bowling along of Prior's vehicle.

An alternative manuscript reading of line 4 is 'On my left hand my Horace, a Nymph on my right'. It may amount to the same thing, but it is worth noting that this is not an expat slumming in a brothel: Prior is not merely open but ostentatious, and he is assuming that the woman at his side is sharing in the let-out-of-school anticipation of an escape from weekday chores. One can also infer that, despite his dislike of Louis's political aims and his contempt for the claque of toadies around the King, Prior would feel more culturally at home in France than in stolid Holland.

This glimpse of him is no doubt accurate, but it is still a composed picture. The category of works which he called 'Amorous Odes' represents him as a participant (usually a rueful one) in a soap opera of copiously varied incidents with a gallery of women – Chloe most often, but with cameos from Phyllis, Flavia, Amynta, Morella, Nanette, Strephonetta and so forth – not one of which can be assumed to be truly autobiographical, but a few of which probably *were*.

Prior wrote his lyrics in a convention that was gradually withering. The classical paraphernalia of Venus, Cupid, and troops of plump cherubs lost its attraction as the century wore on. Likewise, the pastoral, instead of being a standardised set of accessories to frame the narrow, if at times feverishly indulgent, passions of shepherds and shepherdesses, was subsumed into poetry which focused on Nature for its own sake and observed it quite differently.

The poems which express the strongest feeling tend also to look very conventional. Matthew breaking his heart over the coyness or disdain of Chloe (or Celia or Dorinda) is likely to leave most readers' withers unwrung. The sketches which will probably appeal most are those which have at least the appearance of having been developed from a realistic, specific moment. The following poem is written with a typical, rather strenuous (and patronising) drollness, but it is entertaining to see the eagerly talkative and disputatious male simply walked out on, which is not what he is used to:

> AN ODE TO A LADY
>
> I
>
> Spare, generous victor, spare the slave
> Who did unequal war pursue,

That more than triumph he might have
In being overcome by you.

II

In the dispute, whate'er I said,
My heart was by my tongue belied,
And in my looks you might have read
How much I argued on your side.

III

You, far from danger as from fear,
Might have sustained an open fight,
For seldom your opinions err:
Your eyes are always in the right.

IV

Why, fair one, would you not rely
On Reason's force with Beauty's joined?
Could I their prevalence deny,
I must at once be deaf and blind.

V

Alas! Not hoping to subdue,
I only to the sight aspired:
To keep the beauteous foe in view
Was all the glory I desired.

VI

But she, howe'er of victory sure,
Contemns the wreath too long delayed,
And, armed with more immediate power,
Calls cruel silence to her aid.

VII

Deeper to wound, she shuns the fight,
She drops her arms to gain the field,
Secures her conquest by her flight,
And triumphs when she seems to yield.

VIII

> So, when the Parthian turned his steed,
> And from the hostile camp withdrew,
> With cruel skill the backward reed   [arrow]
> He sent, and as he fled he slew.

Here is a situation which seems as authentic as that of Prior and his companion sweeping through The Hague in his carriage:

> Celia and I the other day
> Walked o'er the sandhills to the sea;
> The setting sun adorned the coast,
> His beams entire, his fierceness lost;
> And, on the surface of the deep,
> The winds lay only not asleep.   [i.e. 'all but']
> The nymph did, like the scene, appear
> Serenely pleasant, calmly fair:
> Soft fell her words as flew the air.
> With secret joy I heard her say
> That she would never miss one day
> A walk so fine, a sight so gay.

The lines are nothing special, but it is refreshing to meet a love-lyric beginning with such a simple pleasure as a stroll beside the sea. Why, it might even have happened. But then the weather turns sinister:

> But, oh, the change! The winds grow high,
> Impending tempests charge the sky,
> The lightning flies, the thunder roars,
> And big waves lash the frightened shores.
> Struck with the horror of the sight,
> She turns her head and wings her flight,
> And, trembling, vows she'll ne'er again
> Approach the shore or view the main.

Did *that* really happen? Possibly. Storms are rare in Arcadia, but frequent along the North Sea coast. But then:

> "Once more at least, look back", said I,
> "Thyself in that large glass descry:
> When thou art in good humour dressed,
> When gentle reason rules thy breast,
> The sun, upon the calmest sea,
> Appears not half so bright as thee ..."

And of course the storm mirrors Celia's tendency towards tantrums and tearfulness. The poem is entitled 'The Lady's Looking-Glass', and is, after all, an artificial and rather trite extended metaphor; it is impossible to tell whether it stemmed from a real outing or not.

Erotic poetry is so often saccharine or whining that a jaundiced reaction may be a tonic. Both by temperament, and because he was following a post-Restoration fashion, Prior sometimes adopted a cynical attitude. "Unhand me, sir", a damsel bleats – but this is no innocent rustic being tousled by a lecherous squire in the hay:

CHASTE FLORIMEL

I

"No – I'll endure ten thousand deaths
Ere any further I'll comply.
Oh, Sir! No man on earth that breathes
Had ever yet his hand so high.

II

"Oh! Take your sword and pierce my heart –
Undaunted see me meet the wound;
Oh! Will you act a Tarquin's part?
A second Lucrece you have found."

III

Thus to the pressing Corydon
Poor Florimel, unhappy maid,
Fearing by love to be undone,
In broken, dying accents said.

IV

Delia, who held the conscious door,
[a Latinate use – 'privy to' many similar occasions]
Inspired by truth and brandy, smiled,
Knowing that sixteen months before
Our Lucrece had her second child.

V

"And hark ye, Madam", cried the bawd,
"None of your flights, your high-rope dodging;
Be civil here, or march abroad;
Oblige the squire, or quit the lodging."

VI

"Oh! Have I", Florimel went on,
"Have I then lost my Delia's aid?
Where shall forsaken Virtue run,
If by her friend she is betrayed?

VII

"Oh, curse on empty friendship's name!
Lord, what is all our future view?
Then, dear destroyer of my fame,
Let my last succour be to you.

VIII

"From Delia's rage and Fortune's frown
A wretched lovesick maid deliver;
Oh! Tip me but another crown,
Dear Sir, and make me yours for ever."

A pair of lovers exchange professions of yearning for the simple life, in which each is all in all to the other:

TO A YOUNG GENTLEMAN IN LOVE

"From public noise and factious strife,
From all the busy ills of life,
Take me, my Celia, to thy breast,
And lull my wearied soul to rest;
For ever in this humble cell
Let thee and I, my fair one, dwell:
None enter else, but Love – and he
Shall bar the door and keep the key.
　To painted roofs and shining spires
(Uneasy seats of high desires)
Let the unthinking many crowd
That dare be covetous and proud;
In golden bondage let them wait,

And barter happiness for state.
But oh, my Celia, when thy swain
Desires to see a Court again,
May Heaven around this destined head
The choicest of its curses shed!
To sum up all the rage of Fate
In the two things I dread and hate,
May'st thou be false and I be great."
Thus, on his Celia's panting breast,
Fond Celadon his soul expressed,
While with delight the lovely maid
Received the vows she thus repaid:
  "Hope of my age, joy of my youth,
Blest miracle of love and truth,
All that could e'er be counted mine,
My love and life, long since are thine:
A real joy I never knew
Till I believed thy passion true;
A real grief I ne'er can find
Till thou prov'st perjured or unkind.
Contempt and poverty and care,
['Content' in the 1784 edition]
All we abhor and all we fear,
(Blest with thy presence) I can bear.
Through waters and through flames I'll go,
Sufferer and solace of thy woe;
Trace me some yet unheard-of way
That I thy ardour may repay,
And make my constant passion known
By more than woman yet has done.
  Had I a wish that did not bear
The stamp and image of my dear,
I'd pierce my heart through every vein,
And die to let it out again.
No – Venus shall my witness be
(If Venus ever loved like me),
That for one hour I would not quit
My Shepherd's arms and this retreat
To be the Persian Monarch's bride,
Partner of all his power and pride,
Or rule in regal state above,
Mother of Gods and wife of Jove."
  O happy these of human race!
But soon, alas! our pleasures pass.
He thanked her on his bended knee,
Then drank a quart of milk and tea,

> And, leaving her adored embrace,
> Hastened to Court to beg a place;
> Whilst she, his absence to bemoan,
> The very moment he was gone
> Called Thyrsis from beneath the bed,
> Where all this time he had been hid.
>
> Moral
>
> While men have these ambitious fancies,
> And wanton wenches read romances,
> Our sex will – What? Out with it! – lie,
> And theirs in equal strains reply.
> The moral of the tale I sing
> (A posy for a wedding ring)
> In this short verse will be confined:
> Love is a jest, and vows are wind.

A characteristic device was to shoot down classical motifs by juxtaposing them with modern pragmatism. So the standard Latin love-lyric situation of the lover rooted outside the beloved's door, either braving her bodyguards or patiently eroding her own resistance, is brushed aside in a no-nonsense epigram:

> FATAL LOVE
>
> Poor Hal caught his death standing under a spout,
> Expecting till midnight when Nan would come out;
> But fatal his patience, as cruel the dame,
> And cursed was the weather that quenched the man's
>   flame.
>   Whoe'er thou art that reads these moral lines,
>   Make love at home, and go to bed betimes.   [early]

Much more elaborate is a parody of the Apollo and Daphne story from Ovid's <u>Metamorphoses</u>. The original is a superb example of Ovid's uncanny ability to dart between melodrama, pathos, beauty, irony and farce. Apollo's wooing speech, which proudly displays his extensive portfolio of divine powers, is blurted out on the hoof as he pursues the nymph; no wonder he asks her to slow down a bit (if she does, he will adjust his speed as well so as not to alarm her). Prior translates Apollo's spiel, but punctuates it with a pitiless commentary from his quarry, who is no shrinking violet in panicky retreat but a hard-as-nails sophisticated modern female who just happens to have a river-god as a father, but who is thoroughly versed in the business of using sex as a bargaining counter.

DAPHNE AND APOLLO

Apollo:	Abate, fair fugitive, abate thy speed,
	Dismiss thy fears and turn thy beauteous head;
	With kind regard a panting lover view;
	Less swiftly fly, less swiftly I'll pursue.
	Pathless, alas! and rugged is the ground:
	Some stone may hurt thee, or some thorn may wound.
Daphne:	This care is for himself, as sure as death:
	One mile has put the fellow out of breath.
	He'll never do; I'll lead him the other round.
	Washy he is [with no stamina], perhaps not over-sound.
Apollo:	You fly, alas! not knowing whom you fly.
	Nor ill-bred swain nor rusty [rustic] clown am I:
	I Claros' isle and Tenedos command –
Daphne:	Thank ye, I would not leave my native land.
Apollo:	What is to come by certain arts I know.
Daphne:	Pish! Partridge has as fair pretence as you.
	[a popular astrologer and almanac-compiler]
Apollo:	Behold the beauties of my locks –
Daphne:	A fig!
	That may be counterfeit, a Spanish wig.
	Who cares for all that bush of curling hair,
	Whilst your smooth chin is so extremely bare?
Apollo:	I sing –
Daphne:	That never shall be Daphne's choice.
	Syphacio had an admirable voice.
	[Siface was an Italian singer – but castrato]
Apollo:	Of every herb I tell the mystic power;
	To certain health the patient I restore,
	Sent for, caressed –
Daphne:	Ours is a wholesome air.
	You'd better go to Town and practise there;
	For me, I've no obstructions to remove:
	I'm pretty well – I thank you, Father Jove –
	And physic is a weak ally to love.
Apollo:	For learning famed, fine verses I compose.
Daphne:	So do your brother quacks and brother beaux.
	Memorials [memos] only, and reviews, write [are written in] prose.
Apollo:	From the bent yew I send the pointed reed,

	Sure of its aim, and fatal in its speed –
Daphne:	Then, leaving me, whom sure you would not kill,
	In yonder thicket exercise your skill:
	Shoot there at beasts; but, for the human heart,
	Your cousin Cupid has the only dart.
Apollo:	Yet turn, O beauteous maid, yet deign to hear
	A lovesick deity's impetuous prayer.
	O let me woo thee as thou wouldst be wooed.
Daphne:	First, therefore, don't be so extremely rude:
	Don't tear the hedges down and tread the clover,
	Like an hobgoblin rather than a lover.
	Next, to my father's grotto sometimes come –
	At ebbing tide he always is at home.
	Read the Courant with him [a newspaper], and let him know
	A little politics, how matters go
	Upon his brother-rivers Rhine or Po.
	As any maid or footman comes or goes,
	Pull off your hat and ask how Daphne does;
	These sort of folks will to each other tell
	That you respect me – that, you know, looks well.
	Then if you are, as you pretend, the god
	That rules the day, and much upon the road,
	You'll find a hundred trifles in your way,
	That you may bring one home from Africa:
	Some little rarity, some bird or beast,
	And now and then a jewel from the East –
	A lacquered cabinet, some China ware –
	You have 'em mighty cheap at Pekin Fair.
	Next, *nota bene*, you shall never rove,
	Nor take example by your father Jove.
	Last, for the ease and comfort of my life,
	Make me – Lord, what startles you? – your wife.
	I'm now, they say, sixteen, or something more;
	We mortals seldom live above fourscore –
	Fourscore – you're good at numbers – let us see,
	Seventeen suppose – remaining, sixty-three –
	Aye, in that span of time you'll bury me.
	Meantime, if you have tumult, noise and strife
	(Things not abhorrent to a married life),
	They'll quickly end, you see; what signify
	A few odd years to you that never die?
	And, after all, you're half your time away:
	You know your business takes you up all day;
	And, coming late to bed, you need not fear:

> Whatever noise I make, you'll sleep, my dear.
> Or, if a winter evening should be long,
> Even read your physic-book or make a song.
> Your wife, your steeds, diachalon [a medicinal
>   plaster] and rhyme
> May take up any honest godhead's time.
> Thus, as you like it, you may love again,
> And let another Daphne have her reign.
> Now, love or leave, my dear, retreat or follow –
> I, Daphne (this premised), take thee, Apollo:
> And may I split into ten thousand trees
> If I give up on other terms than these.
>
> She said; but what the amorous god replied,
> So Fate ordained, is to our search denied:
> By rats, alas! the manuscript is ate.
> O cruel banquet which we all regret!
> Bavius [archetype of the hack writer], thy labours must
>   this work restore –
> May thy goodwill be equal to thy power.

The modern girl is also represented by Kitty, who is less knowing than Daphne but just as determined, and eager to catch up, if only she can wriggle away from the parental leading-strings:

THE FEMALE PHAETON

I

> Thus Kitty, beautiful and young,
> And wild as colt untamed,
> Bespoke the fair from whence she sprung,
> With little rage inflamed –

II

> Inflamed with rage at sad restraint
> Which wise mamma ordained,
> And sorely vexed to play the saint
> Whilst wit and beauty reigned:

III

> "Shall I thumb holy books, confined
> With Abigails [maidservants], forsaken?
> Kitty's for other things designed,
> Or I am much mistaken.

IV

"Must Lady Jenny frisk about,
And visit all her cousins?
At balls must she make all the rout
[a pun on 'rout' as social gathering and irresistible conquest]
And bring home hearts by dozens?

V

"What has she better, pray, than I?
What hidden charms to boast?
That all mankind for her should die,
Whilst I am scarce a toast?

VI

"Dearest Mamma, for once let me,
Unchained, my fortune try:
I'll have my earl as well as she,
Or know the reason why.

VII

"I'll soon with Jenny's pride quit score,   [get even]
Make all her lovers fall:
They'll grieve I was not loosed before –
She, I was loosed at all."

VIII

Fondness prevailed, mamma gave way:
Kitty, at heart's desire,
Obtained the chariot for a day,
And set the world on fire.   [hence the title!]

Prior was too equable to be a natural satirist, although in his early writing he thought this was the way to make himself a name. Wit, he later said, should be used as a shield, not a sword. Daphne and Kitty amuse rather than appal him. He was always alert to human absurdity, though, and the triviality of genteel life in London was egregious enough to cause even the mildest-mannered to snort. Mrs Carvel, for example, embarked on married life with her aged husband, determined to live it to the full in the style that Pope, Swift and the Restoration dramatists have familiarised. When she felt really industrious, she might spend the morning shopping:

> But when no very great affair
> Excited her peculiar care,
> She without fail was waked at ten,
> Drank chocolate, then slept again;
> At twelve she rose; with much ado
> Her clothes were huddled on by two;
> Then, "Does my lady dine at home?"
> "Yes, sure – but is the Colonel come?"
> Next, how to spend the afternoon,
> And not come home again too soon:
> The 'Change [Royal Exchange], the City, or the play,
> As each was proper for the day;
> A turn in summer to Hyde Park,
> When it grew tolerably dark.
> Wife's pleasure causes husband's pain –
> Strange fancies come in Hans's brain:
> He thought of what he did not name,
> And would reform, but durst not blame.
> At first he therefore preached his wife
> The comforts of a pious life;
> Told her how transient beauty was;
> That all must die, and flesh was grass.
> He bought her sermons, psalms and graces,
> And doubled down the useful places;
> But still the weight of worldly care
> Allowed her little time for prayer,
> And 'Cleopatra' was read o'er,
>
> [presumably the romance by La Calprenède in translation]
>
> While Scot and Wake, and twenty more,
> That teach one to deny one's self,
> Stood unmolested on the shelf.
>
> [John Scott and William Wake, clergymen and devotional authors – Wake was to become Archbishop of Canterbury]
>
> An untouched Bible graced her toilette –
> No fear that thumb of hers should spoil it.
> In short, the trade was still the same:
> The dame went out, the Colonel came.
> ['Hans Carvel']

This develops into another fabliau, with the sort of gleefully obscene climax which removed Prior's works from the bookshelves of decorous households – never really to make a come-back, which explains the raison d'être of this booklet.

Jealousy, adultery, inconstancy: such things are no joke, yet they are also funny. What Prior expected, just like Donne, was that a collection of erotic lyrics would dramatise the range of emotions and behaviour that being in love provokes. The 'she' can be an ingénue, a coquette, a society lady, a milkmaid or a prostitute; the 'I' can be a rake, the bashful worshipper of a pedestalised goddess, a besotted masochist coming back for yet another repulse, or a long-term partner who is cooling off. It is pointless to speculate whether Prior ever courted a woman like this:

 I

 Since we your husband daily see
 So jealous out of season,
 Phyllis, let you and I agree
 To make him so with reason.

 II

 I'm vexed to think that every night
 A sot, within thy arms
 Tasting the most divine delight,
 Should sully all your charms –

 III

 While, fretting, I must lie alone,
 Cursing the powers divine
 That undeservedly have thrown
 A pearl unto a swine.

 IV

 Then, Phyllis, heal my wounded heart,
 My burning passion cool:
 Let me at least in thee have part
 With thy insipid fool.

 V

 Let him by night his joys pursue,
 And blunder in the dark,
 While I, by day enjoying you,
 Can see to hit the mark.

It is a song, 'Set by Mr Smith' to music. Not quite the subject matter for a Victorian parlour ballad, but it can easily be imagined as a catchy number in a comic operetta.

From Roman poetry to Elizabethan 'citizen comedy' and louche Restoration drama and lyric, that undeserving husband is always the butt, and the more possessively he behaves, the more absurd he appears. Posing as an Ovidian expert in the techniques of adulterous intrigue, Prior offers some unselfish advice which is probably more useful than that given by the Devil when he is consulted by Mr Carvel. His recommended treatment is psychological, and administered in two stages:

> Dear angry friend, what must be done?
> Is there no way? There is but one.
> Send her abroad, and let her see
> That all this mingled mass which she,
> Being forbidden, longs to know
> Is a dull farce, an empty show,
> Powder, and pocket-glass and beau;
> A staple of romance and lies,

[two senses of 'staple' would fit here – 'diet' or 'market']

> False tears and real perjuries ...

The second stage involves the husband more positively:

> Let her behold the frantic scene –
> The women wretched, false the men –
> And when, these certain ills to shun,
> She would to thy embraces run,
> Receive her with extended arms;
> Seem more delighted with her charms;
> Wait on her to the Park and play;
> Put on good humour, make her gay;
> Be to her virtues very kind;
> Be to her faults a little blind;
> Let all her ways be unconfined;
> And clap your Padlock – on her mind.
> ['An English Padlock']

This is more civilised than investing in chastity belts with improved security features. It does, however, rely on the wife sharing Prior's view of the rottenness at the heart of Society's sexual games. It wouldn't work on Mrs Carvel, who plunges joyfully into the farce, and Kitty the Female Phaeton is in no mood yet to be disillusioned by tinsel.

Prior never married, if incontrovertible facts are desired after all the role-playing. He kept serial, long-term mistresses instead. Might one of them have received this little seasonal offering?:

THE NEW-YEAR'S GIFT TO PHYLLIS

I

The circling months begin this day
   To run their yearly ring,
And long-breathed time, which ne'er will stay,
Refits his wings and shoots away,
   It round again to bring.

II

Who feels the force of female eyes,
   And thinks some Nymph divine,
Now brings his annual sacrifice –
Some pretty boy or neat device –
   To offer at her shrine.

III

But I can pay no offering
   To show how I adore,
Since I had but a heart to bring –
A downright foolish, faithful thing –
   And that you had before.

IV

Yet we may give, for custom sake,
   What will to both be new –
My constancy a gift I'll make,
And in return of it will take
   Some levity from you.

The theory of this as a genuine if ironic billet doux (with a false name in the title so that it could one day be published) has to overcome the problem that a reader familiar with Prior's poetry may reasonably observe that levity is more obviously a characteristic of the poet's persona than constancy, so the gifts are of dubious point. Here is Phyllis again, with Mr Smith once more on hand to provide the tune:

I

Phyllis, since we have both been kind,
And of each other had our fill,
Tell me what pleasure you can find
In forcing Nature 'gainst her will.

II

'Tis true, you may with art and pain
Keep in some glowings of desire,
But still those glowings which remain
Are only ashes of the fire.

III

Then let us free each other's soul,
And laugh at the dull, constant fool
Who would Love's liberty control,
And teach us how to whine by rule.

IV

Let us no impositions set
Or clogs upon each other's heart:
But as for pleasure first we met,
So now for pleasure let us part.

V

We both have spent our stock of love,
So consequently should be free;
Thyrsis expects you in yon grove,
And pretty Chloris stays for me.

 A liberating acknowledgment by sensible adults of the loss of momentum in relationships, or Prior making excuses for being a 'love-rat', or a composition based on what he has heard or read of other people's weasellings? An even worse emotional diminuendo is described in this passage, which we know can only be tangentially autobiographical at most, but which embodies a commonplace 18th century view of married life (Mary Leapor saw it the same way from the other side of the breakfast table, and she didn't risk wedlock either):

> And now your matrimonial Cupid,
> Lashed on by Time, grows tired and stupid –
> For story and experience tell us
> That man grows cold and woman jealous.
> Both would their little ends secure:
> He sighs for freedom, she for power:
> His wishes tend abroad to roam,
> And hers to domineer at home.
> Thus passion flags by slow degrees,
> And, ruffled more, delighted less,
> The busy mind does seldom go
> To those once charming seats below;
> But, in the breast encamped, prepares
> For wellbred feints and future wars.
> The man suspects his lady's crying
> (When he last autumn lay a-dying)
> Was but to gain him to appoint her
> By codicil a larger jointure;
> The woman finds it all a trick
> That he could swoon when she was sick,
> And knows that in that grief he reckoned
> On black-eyed Susan for his second.
> ['Alma', II/63-84]

Female readers will be grimly aware that poets are almost certain to expel a melancholy sigh sooner or later and deplore the transience of beauty. Phyllis may boast of robust good health (far better than that of some hypochondriac youngsters she knows), but she is less well than she thinks: 'No lenitives can thy disease assuage: / I tell thee, 'tis incurable – 'tis age.' ['The Incurable']

There are remedies for marital plagues and the cruelty of Time. One is simply to accept the unavoidable vicissitudes of mood, as the elderly couple in 'The Ladle' had done; another is to cultivate a different quality if one is to remain attractive after the man's ardour dwindles – the female reader will probably be expecting this with gritted teeth as well. But even being solicitous and obliging doesn't guarantee success:

> Take heed, my dear, youth flies apace;
> As well as Cupid, Time is blind;
> Soon must those glories of thy face
> The fate of vulgar beauty find:
> The thousand Loves that arm thy potent eye
> Must drop their quivers, flag their wings, and die.

> Then wilt thou sigh, when in each frown
> A hateful wrinkle more appears,
> And putting peevish humours on
> Seems but the sad effect of years.
> Kindness itself too weak a charm will prove
> To raise the feeble fires of aged love.
>
> Forced compliments and formal bows
> Will show thee just above neglect;
> The heat with which thy lover glows
> Will settle into cold respect.
> A talking, dull Platonic I shall turn:
> Learn to be civil when I cease to burn.

The poem teases by amalgamating two literary clichés. One is that, when good looks fade, good nature must compensate (though civility may be all that the partner can muster by then in response); the other is that you make hay or gather rosebuds while you may. So the poem develops into a warning that the young woman should cultivate 'kindness and constancy' immediately, while she still has her best gifts to bestow, not just when she has nothing else to offer:

> Then shun the ill, and know, my dear,
> Kindness and constancy will prove
> The only pillars fit to bear
> So vast a weight as that of love.
> If thou canst wish to make my flames endure,
> Thine must be very fierce and very pure.
>
> Haste, Celia, haste, while youth invites,
> Obey kind Cupid's present voice;
> Fill every sense with soft delights,
> And give thy soul a loose to joys:
> Let millions of repeated blisses prove
> That thou all kindness art, and I all love.
>
> Be mine and only mine; take care
> Thy looks, thy thoughts, thy dreams to guide
> To me alone; nor come so far
> As liking any youth beside;
> What men e'er court thee, fly 'em, and believe
> They're serpents all, and thou the tempted Eve.
>
> So shall I court thy dearest truth,
> When beauty ceases to engage;

> So, thinking on thy charming youth,
> I'll love it o'er again in age.
> So Time itself our raptures shall improve,
> While still we wake to joy and live to love.
> ['An Ode']

The poem may not appeal, and may indeed thoroughly irritate – a typical man's attitude, you may say. But it is surely a *clever* poem, in that it juggles commonplaces rapidly and cheekily, moving between earnestness and flippancy, well aware that it is chopping logic, but nudging Celia and the reader towards its theory, however questionable, of the value and durability of erotic afterglow as the fires of a relationship die down.

Prior was always searching for fresh angles on old literary themes. One of his most exhibitionist performances was 'Henry and Emma' which, after a short period of great popularity, tended to polarise reactions into 'exquisite' and 'imbecilic'. It is an updating of a ballad from about 1500 called 'The Nutbrown Maid', in which a young man informs his sweetheart that he has been banished and must bid her adieu for her own sake. She asserts her resolution to share his exile; he describes its manifold inconveniences; she pooh-poohs them; he caps his warning by telling her that he has someone waiting for him whom he loves better; she assures him that she will be his and her handmaiden rather than forgo proximity to the man she loves best; he tells her that he was just testing, and they can get married in aristocratic comfort now that she has proved her constancy.

It is an ugly tale with some lovely passages in the original. It comes from the same folkloric tradition as the story of Patient Grissill or Griselda told by Chaucer in 'The Clerk's Tale'; he admired the stoicism of the put-upon wife but deplored the itch that drove the husband to impose an unnecessary and sadistic loyalty test. So transparently unsuitable is the tale for remodelling in urbane 18th century couplets that one suspects Prior undertook it after being dared or as a bet with himself. Ludicrous passages abound. Warned that the life of an outlaw lacks civilised amenities, Emma promises to deploy all her aptitude as housekeeper and carer:

> When from the cave thou risest with the day
> To beat the woods and rouse the bounding prey,
> The cave with moss and branches I'll adorn,
> And cheerful sit to wait my lord's return.

> And when thou frequent bring'st the smitten deer
> (For seldom, archers say, thy arrows err),
> I'll fetch quick fuel from the neighbouring wood,
> And strike the sparkling flint, and dress the food;
> With humble duty and officious haste
> I'll cull the furthest mead for thy repast:
> The choicest herbs I to thy board will bring,
> And draw thy water from the freshest spring;
> And when at night, with weary toil oppressed,
> Soft slumbers thou enjoy'st and wholesome rest,
> Watchful I'll guard thee, and with midnight prayer
> Weary the gods to keep thee in their care ...
> ['Henry and Emma', 396-411]

This is reminiscent of Imogen's housewifely skills in the challengingly basic environment of cave life in the Welsh mountains in Cymbeline ('But his neat cookery! he cut our roots in characters ...') – not one of Shakespeare's finest moments, either.

All the same, 'Henry and Emma' painstakingly counters the chauvinistic stereotype of the vain, frivolous, inconstant, selfish woman which peeps out in other poems. Another Medieval convention borrowed (or ambushed) by Prior is the ornithological allegory-debate. 'The Turtle and Sparrow' draws on Chaucer's 'Parliament of Fowls' crossed with the Wife of Bath's Prologue (the sexes having been reversed). The turtle-dove laments her recent bereavement, and the sparrow tries to cheer her up and encourage her to find a new mate by recounting his crowded and tempestuous love-life, which has never deterred him from risking a fresh instalment. Wife number three will serve as an example:

> As yet my fortune was but narrow,
> I wooed my cousin, Philly Sparrow,
> O' the elder house of Chirping-End,
> From whence the younger branch descend.
> Well seated in a field of pease
> She lived, extremely at her ease;
> But when the honeymoon was past,
> The following nights were soon o'ercast:
> She kept her own, could plead the law,
> And quarrel for a barley-straw –
> Both, you may judge, became less kind
> As more we knew each other's mind.
> She soon grew sullen, I hard-hearted;
> We scolded, hated, fought and parted.

> To London, blessed town, I went;
> She boarded at a farm in Kent.
> A magpie from the country fled,
> And kindly told me she was dead;
> I pruned my feathers, cocked my tail,
> And set my heart again to sale.
> [278-297]

He has seen off six and is still in the market, despite this gruesome laddishness:

> My dearest dove, one wise man says,
> Alluding to our present case,
> "We're here today and gone tomorrow";
> Then what avails superfluous sorrow?
> Another full as wise as he
> Adds that "A married man may see
> Two happy hours"; and which are they?
> The first and last, perhaps you'll say:
> 'Tis true, when blithe she goes to bed,
> And when she peaceably lies dead.
> "Women 'twixt sheets are best", 'tis said,
> Be they of holland or of lead.
> [376-87]

The varieties of marital disaster are told in lively fashion, as long as the reader is prepared not to take umbrage at the parade of stereotypes. But I will bypass these in order to reach the splendid anathema pronounced by the unconsoled widow on the incorrigible lecher:

> Thy tale has raised a turtle's spleen.
> Uxorious inmate, bird obscene,
> Dar'st thou defile these sacred groves,
> These silent seats of faithful loves?
> Begone! With flagging wings sit down
> On some old penthouse near the Town;
> In brewers' stables peck thy grain,
> Then wash it down with puddled rain,
> And hear thy dirty offspring squall
> From bottles on a suburb-wall.

[earthenware bottles were put up as 'bird-boxes' for sparrows, whose nestlings then became ingredients in 'sparrow pie']

> Where thou hast been, return again,
> Vile bird. Thou hast conversed with men:
> Notions like these from men are given,

> Those vilest creatures under Heaven.
>   To cities and to courts repair:
> Flattery and falsehood flourish there.
> There all thy wretched arts employ,
> Where riches triumph over joy,
> Where passions do with interest barter,
> And Hymen holds by Mammon's charter,
> Where truth by point of law is parried,
> And knaves and prudes are six times married.
> [418-39]

The effect of this is rhetorically enhanced by the insistence on the avian qualities of the creature which have tended to slip out of the picture that the sparrow himself has drawn in his parodies of human marriage. Then comes the 'Application', addressed to Margaret, the daughter of Edward Harley, Earl of Oxford, and Henrietta Cavendish, close friends of Prior's, at whose house, Wimpole in Cambridgeshire, he was staying when he suddenly fell ill and died:

> O dearest daughter of two dearest friends,
> To thee my Muse this little tale commends.
> Loving and loved, regard thy future mate,
> Long love his person, though deplore his fate.
> Seem young when old in thy dear husband's arms,
> For constant virtue has immortal charms;
> And when I lie low, sepulchred in earth,
> And the glad year returns thy day of birth,
> Vouchsafe to say, "Ere I could write or spell,
> The bard who from my cradle wished me well
> Told me I should the prating sparrow blame,
> And bid me imitate the turtle's flame."
> [440-451]

That is the 'real' Prior, at least as much as the wit, the cynic and the chauvinist. He wrote some rollicking, self-consciously smart and show-off verse epistles to adults, but he produced a very improving, scaled-down, but resonantly-titled composition to the same little girl:

> A LETTER TO THE HONOURABLE LADY, MISS
> MARGARET-CAVENDISH-HOLLES-HARLEY
>
> My noble, lovely, little Peggy,
> Let this, my first epistle, beg ye,
> At dawn of morn, and close of even,

To lift your heart and hands to Heaven.
In double beauty say your prayer:
Our father first, then *Notre père*.
And, dearest child, along the day,
In everything you do and say,
Obey and please my Lord and Lady,
So God shall love, and Angels aid ye.

If to these precepts you attend,
No second letter need I send,
And so I rest your constant Friend,
                                                    M.P.

He was right to pay attention to her – far more than he could have known. She was to become one of the most notable Englishwomen of the century, and her collecting passion made his accumulations shrink to the equivalent of a child's stash of coloured pebbles. Perhaps she did take 'The Turtle and Sparrow' to heart: she didn't remarry after the death of William Bentinck, Duke of Portland, who was her husband for 27 years.

In passing, it seems a pity that Prior never had a child – or, at any rate, one that was known about and acknowledged. Men who were interested in, or comfortable with, children were not conspicuously common at that time, but Prior regarded them with affection and amusement. His rejection of the theories that the soul was located in the brain or diffused through the whole body led him to propound an alternative, that it migrated through different regions as the human grew, beginning at the base and moving upwards:

> First, I demonstratively prove
> That feet were only made to move,
> And legs desire to come and go,
> For they have nothing else to do.
>   Hence, long before the child can crawl,
> He learns to kick, and wince, and sprawl:
> To hinder which, your midwife knows
> To bind those parts extremely close,
> Lest Alma, newly entered in,
> And stunned at her own christening's din,
> Fearful of future grief and pain,
> Should silently sneak out again.
> Full piteous seems young Alma's case:
> As in a luckless gamester's place,
> She would not play, yet must not pass.

> Again, as she grows something stronger,
> And master's feet are swathed no longer,
> If in the night too oft he kicks,
> Or shows his locomotive tricks,
> These first assaults fat Kate repays him, [the nursemaid]
> When, half-asleep, she overlays him.
>   Now mark, dear Richard, from the age
> That children tread this worldly stage,
> Broomstaff or poker they bestride,
> And round the parlour love to ride,
> Till thoughtful father's pious care
> Provides his brood, next Smithfield Fair,
> With supplemental hobbyhorses,
> And happy be their infant courses!
>   Hence for some years they ne'er stand still:
> Their legs, you see, direct their will.
> From opening morn till setting sun,
> Around the fields and woods they run;
> They frisk, and dance, and leap, and play,
> Nor heed what Freind or Snape can say.
> [Andrew Snape, clergyman and Headmaster of Eton; Robert Freind, also clergyman and Headmaster of Westminster, Prior's old school]
>   ['Alma', I/270-304]

Alma's next stage is moving up to the thighs, as older children become interested in sport:

> While Betty dances on the green,
> And Susan is at stoolball seen;
> While John for ninepins does declare,
> And Roger loves to pitch the bar ...
> [I/309-12]

From there, naturally, the soul ascends to the groin as puberty changes a young person's focus – and at this point, Prior's friend erupts in protest. Surely love is located in 'A higher place than you assigned him', such as the heart or the liver, the traditional seat of the passions. Poetic slush, Prior replies:

> But let your friends in verse suppose
> What ne'er shall be allowed in prose,
> Anatomists can make it clear
> The liver minds its own affair,
> Kindly supplies our public uses,
> And parts and strains the vital juices ...   [I/435-40]

And the heart is the seat of courage, so how can it have room for sentiment? This is not serious metaphysics, of course. 'Alma' is the work of a philosophical addict at play. But if Prior wears a heart on his sleeve in his poetry, it would be advisable to suspect that it may be a simulacrum.

In his *own* heart, he knew the difference perfectly well between literary games and the real thing, even though it amused him (and, I hope, you) to juggle ingeniously with the former. How to be sure? Quite simply, this poem, written as a tribute to one of his mistresses, Jane Ansley, 'Jinny' (we probably met her in that carriage):

> Released from the noise of the butcher and baker,
> Who, my old friends be thanked, did seldom forsake her,
> And from the soft duns of my landlord, the Quaker;
>
> From chiding the footmen and watching the lasses,
> From Nell that burned milk, and Tom that broke glasses
> (Sad mischiefs through which a good housekeeper
>   passes!);
>
> From some real care, but more fancied vexation,
> From a life parti-coloured, half reason, half passion,
> Here lies after all the best wench in the nation.
>
> From the Rhine to the Po, from the Thames to the
>   Rhone,
> Joanna or Janneton, Jinny or Joan –
> 'Twas all one to her by what name she was known:
>
> For the idiom of words very little she heeded,
> Provided the matter she drove at succeeded:
> She took and gave languages just as she needed.
>
> So for kitchen and market, for bargain and sale,
> She paid English or Dutch or French down on the nail,
> But in telling a story she sometimes did fail –
>
> Then, begging excuse as she happened to stammer,
> With respect to her betters, but none to her grammar,
> Her blush helped her out, and her jargon became her.
>
> Her habit and mien she endeavoured to frame
> To the different *goût* of the place where she came –
> Her outside still changed, but her inside the same:

At The Hague in her slippers, and hair as the mode is;
At Paris all 'falbalowed' fine as a goddess;
[Prior's version of 'furbelowed', decorated with flounces]
And at censuring London in a smock sleeves and bodice.

She ordered affairs that few people could tell
In what part about her that mixture did dwell
Of Vrouw or Mistress or Mademoiselle.

For her surname and race, let the Heralds e'en answer;
Her own proper worth was enough to advance her,
And he who liked her little valued her grandsire;

But from what House soever her lineage may come,
I wish my own Jinny but out of her tomb,
Though all her relations were there in her room.

Of such terrible beauty she never could boast
As with absolute sway o'er all hearts rules the roast,
When J--- bawls out to the Chair for a toast;

But of good household features her person was made,
Nor by faction cried up nor of censure afraid,
And her beauty was rather for use than parade;

Her blood so well mixed, and flesh so well pasted,
That, though her youth faded, her comeliness lasted –
The blue was wore off, but the plum was well tasted;

Less smooth than her skin and less white than her breast
Was this polished stone beneath which she lies pressed;
Stop, reader, and sigh, while thou thinkst on the rest.

With a just trim of virtue her soul was endued:
Not affectedly pious nor secretly lewd,
She cut even between the coquette and the prude.

Her will with her duty so equally stood
That, seldom opposed, she was commonly good,
And did pretty well, doing just what she would.

Declining all power, she found means to persuade:
Was then most regarded when most she obeyed –
The Mistress, in truth, when she seemed but the Maid.

Such care of her own proper actions she took
That on other folks' lives she had no time to look,
So censure and praise were struck out of her book;

Her thought still confined to its own little sphere,
She minded not who did excel or did err,
But just as the matter related to her.

Then, too, when her private tribunal was reared,
Her mercy so mixed with her judgment appeared
That her foes were condemned and her friends always
                                                  cleared.

Her religion so well with her learning did suit
That, in practice sincere and in controverse mute,
She showed she knew better to live than dispute;

Some parts of the Bible by heart she recited,
And much in historical chapters delighted,
But in points about faith she was something short-
                                                  sighted:

So notions and modes she referred to the Schools,
And in matters of conscience adhered to two rules:
To advise with no bigots, and jest with no fools;

And, scrupling but little, enough she believed;
By charity, ample small sins she retrieved,
And when she had new clothes, she always received.

Thus still whilst her morning unseen fled away,
In ordering the linen and making the tea,
That she scarce could have time for the Psalms of the
                                                  Day;

And while after dinner the night came so soon
That half she proposed very seldom was done,
With twenty "God bless me"s, "How this day is gone!";

While she read and accounted and paid and abated,
Eat and drank, played and worked, laughed and cried,
                                        loved and hated,
As answered the end of her being created;

In the midst of her age came a cruel disease
Which neither her juleps nor receipts could appease,
So down dropped her clay – may her soul be at peace.

Retire from this sepulchre, all the profane –
You that love for debauch or that marry for gain –
Retire lest ye trouble the Manes of J--- ; [spirit]

But thou that know'st love above interest or lust,
Strew the myrtle and rose on this once-beloved dust,
And shed one pious tear upon Jinny the Just;

Tread soft on her grave, and do right to her honour;
Let neither rude hand nor ill tongue light upon her;
Do all the small favours that now can be done her;

And when what thou liked shall return to her clay –
For so I'm persuaded she must do one day,
Whatever fantastic J---- Asgil may say –
[John Asgill wrote a pamphlet to prove that Christians could be translated into eternal life without having to die first]

When, as I have done now, thou shalt set up a stone
For something, however distinguished or known –
May some pious friend the misfortune bemoan,
And make thy concern, by reflection, his own.

'Jinny the Just', which exists only in manuscript, untitled, is unique. Henry Fielding would have loved this portrait, but even he could not have done it better. Has a more vivid and touching one been created in verse? Here at least is the real thing. Jinny and Matt.

A NATURAL INTERLUDE

Prior was intrigued by the natural world, but it was an intellectual sort of curiosity. In an early poem written at Cambridge, he began at the apex:

> Why does the constant sun
> With measured steps his radiant journeys run?
> Why does he order the diurnal hours
> To leave earth's other part and rise in ours?
> Why does he wake the correspondent moon
> And fill her willing lamp with liquid light,
> Commanding her, with delegated powers,
> To beautify the world and bless the night?
> Why does each animated star
> Love the just limits of its proper sphere?
> Why does each consenting sign [of the zodiac]
> With prudent harmony combine
> In turns to move, and subsequent appear,
> To gird the globe and regulate the year?
> ['An Ode on Exodus iii.14']

Many years later, he showed Solomon puzzling over less ethereal scientific questions:

> I know not why the beech delights the glade,
> With boughs extended and a rounder shade,
> Whilst towering firs in conic forms arise,
> And with a pointed spear divide the skies;
> Nor why again the changing oak should shed
> The yearly honour of his stately head,
> Whilst the distinguished yew is ever seen
> Unchanged his branch and permanent his green;
> Wanting the sun, why does the caltha fade?
> Why does the cypress flourish in the shade?
> The fig and date, why love they to remain
> In middle station and an even plain,
> While in the lower marsh the gourd is found,
> And while the hill with olive-shade is crowned?
> Why does one climate and one soil endue
> The blushing poppy with a crimson hue,
> Yet leave the lily pale, and tinge the violet blue?
> Why does the fond carnation love to shoot
> A various colour from one parent root,
> While the fantastic tulip strives to break

> In twofold beauty and a parted streak?
> The twining jasmine and the blushing rose
> With lavish grace their morning scents disclose;
> The smelling tuberose and jonquil declare
> The stronger impulse of an evening air.
> Whence has the tree (resolve me) or the flower
> A various instinct or a different power?
> Why should one earth, one clime, one stream, one breath,
> Raise this to strength and sicken that to death?
> Whence does it happen that the plant, which well
> We name the sensitive, should move and feel?
> Whence know her leaves to answer her command,
> And with quick horror fly the neighbouring hand?
> ['Solomon', I/57-89]

The ways of birds, beasts and fish worry him, too. He experiences a rather Darwinian moment, without pursuing the conundrums he raises:

> In foreign isles which our discoverers find,
> Far from this length of continent disjoined,
> The rugged bear's or spotted lynx's brood
> Frighten the valleys and infest the wood,
> The hungry crocodile and hissing snake
> Lurk in the troubled stream and fenny brake;
> And man, untaught, and ravenous as the beast,
> Does valley, wood, and brake, and stream infest.
> Derived these men and animals their birth
> From trunk of oak or pregnant womb of earth?
> Whence then the old belief that all began
> In Eden's shade and one created man?
> Or grant this progeny was wafted o'er
> By coasting boats from next adjacent shore,
> Would those, from whom we will suppose they spring,
> Slaughter to harmless lands and poison bring?
> Would they on board or bears or lynxes take,
> Feed the she-adder and the brooding snake?
> [I/319-36]

'Alma' reveals that the poet still has many problems buzzing round in his mind ('The brain contains ten thousand cells, / In each some active fancy dwells'), but they sound less metaphysically upsetting in the jaunty octosyllabics that the poem is written in:

> Faith, Dick, I must confess 'tis true
> (But this is only *entre nous*)
> That many knotty points there are
> Which all discuss but few can clear;
> As Nature slyly had thought fit,
> For some by-ends, to crossbite wit: [cheat]
> Circles to square and cubes to double
> Would give a man excessive trouble;
> The longitude uncertain roams
> In spite of Wh----n and his bombs.

[William Whiston, a controversial theologian and a mathematician with a special interest in determining a ship's longitude]

> What System, Dick, has right averred
> The cause why woman has no beard?
> Or why, as years our frame attack,
> Our hair grows white, our teeth grow black?
> In points like these, we must agree
> Our barber knows as much as we,
> Yet, still unable to explain,
> We must persist the best we can;
> With care our Systems still renew,
> And prove things likely, though not true.
> ['Alma', III/360-79]

The parlour game of guessing the rationale behind Creation indicates a lightly scientific interest, but not an Arcadian sentimentality about Nature. Prior tinkered with the pastoral as a literary genre, but, as usual, saw it as a long-established poetic resource to mimic or parody. At the age of 25, he seemed less than thrilled by the humdrum routine of country life:

> For me, whom wandering Fortune threw
> From what I loved, the Town and you,
> Let me just tell you how my time is
> Passed in a country life – *Imprimis*,   [first of all]
> As soon as Phoebus' rays inspect us,
> First, Sir, I read, and then I breakfast;
> So on, till foresaid god does set –
> I sometimes study, sometimes eat ...
> Sometimes I climb my mare, and kick her
> To bottled ale and neighbouring vicar ...
> Thus, without much delight or grief,
> I fool away an idle life ...
> ['An Epistle to Fleetwood Shephard', May 1689]

All the same, it would have needed rugged scepticism to avoid altogether the almost universal assumption, in poetry at least, that all life's worries and frustrations would disappear if only a commitment could be made to that paradisal retreat where one would lead the simple life surrounded by bubbling rills and flower-enamelled meadows – not forgetting a well-stocked library and cellar.

In mid-career, under a good deal of stress, he succumbed to the fantasy, responding ambivalently to the dazzling vision of the world's diversity which he had recently read, and addressing Rhea, the daughter of Earth and Sky, mother of Zeus, and embodiment of Nature:

> WRITTEN AT PARIS 1700, IN THE BEGINNING OF ROBE'S GEOGRAPHY
>
> Of all that William rules, or Robe
> Describes, great Rhea, of thy globe,
> When, or on posthorse or in chaise,
> With much expense and little ease
> My destined miles I shall have gone,
> By Thames or Maese [Meuse], by Po or Rhone,
> And found no foot of earth my own:
> Great Mother, let me once be able
> To have a garden, house and stable,
> That I may read and ride and plant,
> Superior to desire or want;
> And, as health fails and years increase,
> Sit down and think, and die in peace.
> Oblige thy favourite undertakers   [executives]
> To throw me in but twenty acres:
> This number, sure, they may allow –
> For pasture ten, and ten for plough –
> 'Tis all that I would wish or hope,
> For me, and John, and Nell, and Crop.
> [his servants and horse]
>   Then, as thou wilt, dispose the rest
> (And let not Fortune spoil the jest)
> To those who at the market rate
> Can barter honour for estate.
>   Now, if thou grant'st me my request,
> To make thy votary truly blest
> Let curst Revenge and saucy Pride
> To some bleak rock far off be tied,
> Nor e'er approach my rural seat

To tempt me to be base and great.
  And, Goddess, this kind office done,
Charge Venus to command her son
(Wherever else she lets him rove)
To shun my house and field and grove:
Peace cannot dwell with Hate or Love.
  Hear, gracious Rhea, what I say,
And thy petitioner shall pray.

As we have already seen in 'The Ladle', the trouble with asking for boons is that they might be granted. After the Whig administration had finished his career, there was no serious obstacle, once he had re-stabilised his finances (with Harley's help), to fulfilling the dream, so he contacted the Top People's estate agent, John Morley, and off they went to inspect a property in Essex called Down Hall. The journey was transformed into a miniature mock-epic odyssey:

> DOWN-HALL. A BALLAD. To the tune of 'King John and the Abbot of Canterbury'. Written in the year 1715.
>
> I
>
> I sing not old Jason who travelled through Greece
> To kiss the fair maids and possess the rich fleece,
> Nor sing I Aeneas who, led by his mother [Venus],
> Got rid of one wife and went far for another,
> [Dido and Lavinia]
> Derry down, down, hey derry down.
>
> II
>
> Nor him who through Asia and Europe did roam,
> Ulysses by name, who ne'er cared to go home,
> But rather desired to see cities and men
> Than return to his farms and converse with old Pen,
> [his wife, Penelope!]
> Derry down &c.
>
> III
>
> Hang Homer and Virgil! Their meaning to seek,
> A man must have poked into Latin and Greek;
> Those who love their own tongue, we have reason to hope,
> Have read them translated by Dryden and Pope,
> Derry down &c.

IV

But I sing of exploits that have lately been done
By two British heroes called Matthew and John,
And how they rid friendly from fine London town
Fair Essex to see, and a place they call Down,
Derry down &c.

V

Now, ere they went out, you may rightly suppose
How much they discoursed both in prudence and prose:
For before this great journey was throughly concerted,
Full often they met, and as often they parted,
Derry down &c.

VI

And thus Matthew said, "Look you here, my friend John,
I fairly have travelled years thirty and one,
And though I still carried my Sovereign's warrant,
I only have gone upon other folks' errands,
Derry down &c.

VII

"And now in this journey of life I would have
A place where to bait 'twixt the Court and the grave,
['bait' is 'to take refreshment', as in dialect still]
Where joyful to live, not unwilling to die –"
"Gadzooks! I have just such a place in my eye,
Derry down &c.

VIII

"There are gardens so stately, and arbours so thick,
A portal of stone, and a fabric of brick;
The matter next week shall be all in your power –
But the money, Gadzooks! must be paid in an hour,
Derry down &c.

IX

"For things in this world must by law be made certain:
We both must repair unto Oliver Martin,
For he is a lawyer of worthy renown –

I'll bring you to see he must fix you at Down",
Derry down &c.

X

Quoth Matthew, "I know that, from Berwick to Dover,
You've sold all your premises over and over;
And now, if your buyers and sellers agree,
You may throw all our acres into the South-Sea,
[the current yardstick of all failed speculations]
Derry down &c.

XI

"But a word to the purpose: tomorrow, dear friend,
We'll see what tonight you so highly commend,
And if with a garden and house I am blest,
Let the Devil and Coninsby go with the rest,
[for Lord Coningsby, see p.22]
Derry down &c.

XII

Then answered Squire Morley, "Pray, get a calash
[a carriage with a folding hood]
That in summer may burn and in winter may splash;
I love dirt and dust; and 'tis always my pleasure
To take with me much of the soil that I measure",
Derry down &c.

XIII

But Matthew thought better, for Matthew thought right,
And hired a chariot so trim and so tight,
That extremes both of winter and summer might pass,
For one window was canvas, the other was glass,
Derry down &c.

XIV

"Draw up!" quoth friend Matthew; "Pull down!" quoth
              friend John,
"We shall be both hotter and colder anon."
Thus talking and scolding, they forward did speed,
And Ralpho paced by under Newman the Swede,

['John Oeman or Newman' was left £50 and a year's wages in Prior's will]
>Derry down &c.

XV

>Into an old inn did this equipage roll,
>At a town they call Hoddesdon, the sign of the Bull,
>Near a nymph with an urn that divides the highway,
>And into a puddle throws mother of tea,
>Derry down &c.

[The Bull was demolished in the 1960s – lines 3 & 4 are more opaque to me ...]

XVI

>"Come here, my sweet landlady, pray, how d'ye do?
>Where is Cecily so cleanly, and Prudence, and Sue?
>And where is the widow that dwelt here below?
>And the hostler that sung about eight years ago?
>Derry down &c.

XVII

>"And where is your sister, so mild and so dear?
>Whose voice to her maids like a trumpet was clear."
>"By my troth", she replies, "you grow younger, I think –
>And pray, Sir, what wine does the gentleman drink?
>Derry down &c.

XVIII

>"Why now, let me die, Sir, or live upon trust,
>If I know to which question to answer you first.
>Why, things since I saw you most strangely have varied:
>The hostler is hanged and the widow is married,
>Derry down &c

XIX

>"And Prue left a child for the parish to nurse,
>And Cecily went off with a gentleman's purse;
>And as to my sister, so mild and so dear,
>She has lain in the churchyard full many a year",
>Derry down &c.

XX

"Well, peace to her ashes – what signifies grief?
She roasted red veal, and she powdered lean beef;
Full nicely she knew to cook up a fine dish,
For tough was her pullets and tender her fish",
Derry down &c.

XXI

"For that matter, Sir, be ye squire, knight or lord,
I'll give you whate'er a good inn can afford;
I should look on myself as unhappily sped
Did I yield to a sister or living or dead,
Derry down &c.

XXII

"Of mutton a delicate neck and a breast
Shall swim in the water in which they were dressed;
And because you great folks are with rarities taken,
Addle-eggs shall be next course, to stup (?) with rank
                                                    bacon,"
Derry down &c.

XXIII

Then supper was served, and the sheets they were laid,
And Morley most lovingly whispered the maid.
The maid! Was she handsome? Why, truly, so-so:
But what Morley whispered we never shall know,
Derry down &c.

XXIV

Then up rose these heroes as brisk as the sun,
And their horses, like his, were prepared to run.
Now when in the morning Matt asked for the score,
John kindly had paid it the evening before,
Derry down &c.

XXV

Their breakfast so warm, to be sure, they did eat,
A custom in travellers mighty discreet;

And thus with great friendship and glee they went on
To find out the place you shall hear of anon,
Called Down, Down, hey derry down.

XXVI

But what did they talk of from morning till noon?
Why, of spots in the sun, and the man in the moon;
Of the Czar's gentle temper, the Stocks in the City,
The wise men of Greece, and the Secret Committee,
Derry down &c.

[the Secret Committee was set up to prepare the impeachment of members and associates of the ousted Tory government, including Prior]

XXVII

So to Harlow they came, and "Hey! Where are you all?
Show us into the parlour, and mind when I call.
Why, your maids have no motion, your men have no life.
Well, master, I hear you have buried your wife,
Derry down &c.

XXVIII

"Come this very instant, take care to provide
Tea, sugar and toast, and a horse and a guide.
Are the Harrisons here, both the old and the young?
And where stands fair Down, the delight of my song?",
Derry down &c.

XXIX

"O Squire, to the grief of my heart I may say,
I have buried two wives since you travelled this way;
And the Harrisons both may be presently here;
And Down stands, I think, where it stood the last year",
Derry down &c.

XXX

Then Joan brought the teapot, and Caleb the toast,
And the wine was frothed out by the hand of mine host;
But we cleared our extempore banquet so fast,
That the Harrisons both were forgot in the haste,
Derry down &c.

XXXI

Now hey for Down-Hall, for the guide he was got;
The chariot was mounted, the horses did trot;
The guide he did bring us a dozen miles round;
But oh! all in vain, for no Down could be found,
Derry down &c.

XXXII

"O thou Popish guide, thou hast led us astray!"
Says he, "How the devil should I know the way?
I never yet travelled this road in my life –
But Down lies on the left, I was told by my wife,"
Derry down &c.

XXXIII

"Thy wife", answered Matthew, "when she went abroad,
Ne'er told thee of half the by-ways she had trod –
Perhaps she met friends, and brought pence to thy
                                             house,
But thou shalt go home without ever a sous [sou -
                                             penny],
Derry down, &c.

XXXIV

"What is this thing, Morley, and how can you mean it?
We have lost our estate here before we have seen it."
"Have patience!", soft Morley in anger replied,
"To find out our way, let us send off our guide,
Derry down &c.

XXXV

"O, here I spy Down! Cast your eye to the west
Where a windmill so stately stands plainly confessed."
"On the west!", replied Matthew, "No windmill I find –
As well thou mayst tell me I see the west wind,
Derry down &c.

XXXVI

"Now pardon me, Morley – the windmill I spy,
But, faithful Achates, no house is there nigh."

[companion of Aeneas, an archetype of loyal friendship]
    "Look again", says mild Morley, "Gadzooks! you are blind!
The mill stands before, and the house lies behind",
Derry down &c.

XXXVII

"O, now a low ruined white shed I discern,
Untiled and unglazed – I believe 'tis a barn."
"A barn! Why, you rave – 'tis a house for a squire,
A justice of peace, or a knight of our shire",
Derry down &c.

XXXVIII

"A house should be built or with brick or with stone."
"Why, 'tis plaster and lath, and I think that's all one:
And such as it is, it has stood with great fame,
Been called a Hall, and has given its name
To Down, Down, hey derry down."

XXXIX

"O Morley, O Morley, if that be a Hall,
The same with the building will suddenly fall –"
"With your friend Jemmy Gibbs about buildings agree,
[James Gibbs the architect, who designed Prior's memorial]
My business is land, and it matters not me,
Derry down &c.

XL

"I wish you could tell what a deuce your head ails –
I showed you Down-Hall, did you look for Versailles?
Then take house and farm as John Ballet will let ye,
For better for worse, as I took my dame, Betty,
Derry down &c.

XLI

"And now, Sir, a word to the wise is enough:
You'll make very little of all your old stuff,
And to build at your age, by my troth, you grow simple –
Are you young and rich like the master of Wimpole?
Derry down &c.

XLII

"If you have these whims of apartments and gardens,
From twice fifty acres you'll near see five farthings;
                                                    ['ne'er'?]
And in yours I shall find the true gentleman's fate –
Ere you finish your house, you'll have spent your
                                                    estate",
Derry down &c.

XLIII

"Now let us touch thumbs, and be friends ere we part.
Here, John, is my thumb." "And here, Matt, is my heart.
To Halstead I speed, and you go back to Town."
Thus ends the first part of the ballad of Down,
Derry down, down, hey derry down.

The circumstantial account of their stopovers shows that Prior had not forgotten that, but for the Grace of God (and the freakishly fortunate patronage of the Earl of Dorset, who found a potboy able to translate Horace), he might himself have been hobnobbing daily with grooms and waitresses rather than literary VIPs and the crowned heads of Europe.

Despite discovering that estate agents very occasionally misrepresent their properties, Prior did indeed buy Down Hall eventually from John Ballet – and died the following year, before he had the chance to beggar himself with grandiose schemes as Morley had predicted. Down Hall is now a palatial country house hotel, heavily rebuilt from the Elizabethan manor house that Prior saw and pretended to be unimpressed by.

He was therefore baulked of his dream of becoming a land-owning grandee. But perhaps his greatest sadness was not to have been an Eskimo. Solomon speculates that the 'quotidian change of heaven' which rushes us from light to dark almost without allowing us to draw breath might be fruitfully exchanged for the weather in the land of the midnight sun, where in summer one can undertake long journeys and projects without the interruption of being benighted, while the winter, which seems at first sight to be so dreary, affords an unexceptionable excuse to enjoy home comforts and become reacquainted with the partner of one's heart's delight:

> And when declining day forsakes their sky,
> When gathering clouds speak gloomy winter nigh,
> With plenty for the coming season blessed,
> Six solid months (an age) they live, released
> From all the labour, process, clamour, woe
> Which our sad scenes of daily action know.
> They light the shining lamp, prepare the feast,
> And with full mirth receive the welcome guest,
> Or tell their tender loves (the only care
> Which now they suffer) to the listening fair;
> And, raised in pleasure or reposed in ease
> (Grateful alternates of substantial peace),
> They bless the long nocturnal influence shed
> On the crowned goblet and the genial bed.
> [I/305-318]

Down Hall seems to be a poor substitute for an igloo.

ASKING THE BIG QUESTIONS

What can be inferred about Prior's view of the clergy? One prejudice took root early on:

> So at pure barn of loud Non-con,
> Where with my grannam I have gone,
> When Lobb had sifted all his text,
> And I well hoped the pudding next,
> Now to apply has plagued me more
> Than all his villain cant before.
> ['An Epistle to Fleetwood Shephard', May 1689]

The young worshipper, looking forward to Sunday dinner, failed to be edified by the Spirit descending upon the dissenting preacher who was humbler in his origins than his self-esteem.

A tittupping anapaestic metre, composed to fit the same tune as that which 'Down Hall' is modelled on (you can supply the 'Derry downs'), is employed to show the Catholic priest in action, dealing with one of those ticklish eleventh-hour despatchings, when the noose gives special urgency and piquancy to the situation:

> "What frightens you thus, my good son?" says the priest;
> "You murdered, are sorry, and have been confessed."
> "O Father! my sorrow will scarce save my bacon,
> For 'twas not that I murdered but that I was taken."
>
> "Pooh! Prithee, ne'er trouble thy head with such fancies;
> Rely on the aid you shall have from Saint Francis;
> If the money you promised be brought to the chest,
> You have only to die – let the Church do the rest.
>
> "And what will folks say if they see you afraid?
> It reflects upon me, as I knew not my trade.
> Courage, friend! Today is your period of sorrow,
> And things will go better, believe me, tomorrow."
>
> "Tomorrow!", our hero replied, in a fright.
> "He that's hanged before noon ought to think of tonight."

> "Tell your beads", quoth the priest, "and be fairly trussed up,
> For you surely tonight shall in Paradise sup."
>
> "Alas!", quoth the Squire, "howe'er sumptuous the treat,
> Parbleu! I shall have little stomach to eat;
> I should therefore esteem it great favour and grace
> Would you be so kind as to go in my place."
>
> "That I would", quoth the Father, "and thank you to boot,
> But our actions, you know, with our duty must suit:
> The feast I proposed to you I cannot taste,
> For this night, by our Order, is marked for a fast."
>
> Then, turning about to the hangman, he said,
> "Dispatch me, I prithee, this troublesome blade,
> For thy cord and my cord both equally tie,
> And we live by the gold for which other men die."
> ['The Thief and Cordelier']

Prior's constitution was not that of a zealot. Whatever he thought of the doctrines of any sect vehemently maintained by its adherents, the observation which he made in 'Alma' typifies his controlled, quizzical objectivity. It says nothing clear about religious truth, but it says a great deal about the quarrelsome extremes of human behaviour, that a relatively small patch of Western Europe should have grown two such antithetical creeds:

> Dick, you love maps, and may perceive
> Rome not far distant from Geneve.
> If the good Pope remains at home,
> He's the first Prince in Christendom.
> Choose then, good Pope, at home to stay,
> Nor westward, curious, take thy way;
> Thy way, unhappy, shouldst thou take
> From Tiber's bank to Leman Lake,
> Thou art an aged priest no more,
> But a young, flaring, painted whore:
> Thy sex is lost; thy town is gone;
> No longer Rome, but Babylon.
> That some few leagues should make this change,
> To men unlearn'd seems mighty strange.
> [II/509-22]

The Established Church seems not to be quite the golden mean between the two. A manuscript fragment finds its deliberations eccentric:

> I learn to think no precept strange
>   That Convocation can propose,
> Nor ever wish nor seek for change
>   Except in mistresses and clothes.

He airs standard complaints, which explain his granny's preference for Mr Lobb and anticipate Mr Wesley:

> Are there not bells in every steeple
> To summon in the docile people?
> And Deans and Prebends, whose great care
> Some two and fifty times a year
> Should to their parish gravely read?
> But if they send them in their stead
> Some curate who can hardly spell,
> This, some conceive, does e'en as well.

Those were fragmentary sarcastic barbs in manuscript, but this epigram is the finished, published article:

THE INSATIABLE PRIEST

I

> Luke Preachill admires [wonders] what we laymen can mean,
> That thus by our profit and pleasure are swayed;
> He has but three livings, and would be a Dean;
> His wife died this year, he has married his maid.

II

> To suppress all his carnal desires in their birth,
> At all hours a lusty young hussy is near;
> And to take off his thoughts from the things of this earth
> He can be content with two thousand a year.

It's cheap and a bit clumsy, but Prior was obviously itching to say it.

Prior's convictions are obscured by drifting clouds of scepticism and disputatiousness. He comments on the difficulties of interpreting Biblical text riddled with metaphor and unreliably transmitted:

> ... no further mortal man can know,
> Than as from Scripture God has deigned to show.
> Here too we find the mighty problem laid
> In mystic darkness and prophetic shade:
> Penned by the poets' rage and breast enlarged,
> Adorned with emblems, and with figures charged;
> Formed to the lyre, and fitted to be sung
> To proper measures of the Hebrew tongue;
> By time corrupt, at first however pure;
> And by translation rendered more obscure;
> By Sects eluded and by Schools perplexed,
> Till in the Comment we involve the Text.

The poem from which the above extract has been taken shows a determination, nevertheless, to struggle both intellectually and emotionally with certain aspects of doctrine. Prior launched himself into what was intended to be an exposition of one of the more contentious, baffling and apparently self-contradictory areas of theology. It was to be called 'Predestination', and it begins with ringing assertiveness. The first question marks appear in lines 23-4: 'Why was I then of my sole guide bereft? / And why to error and amazement left?' After that, they tumble over each other, and after a few pages the coherent sequentiality of the poem disintegrates into random jottings. If the post-mortem transcript is to be credited, Prior began this at Wimpole in August 1721; it is hardly surprising that he progressed no further, then, since he was dead by the middle of the following month. One might wonder, though, if he could ever have finished it. Far from being a magisterial guide to enlighten the confused, it is a dogged, valiant attempt to think things through for himself on paper.

'Predestination', had the shears of Fate not terminated it so irresistibly, could not have maintained Prior's characteristic fall-back position, which was to stress the unknowableness of God's Will. As a smart young student, he rather gleefully scoffed at the presumption of intellectual theorising:

> With daring pride and insolent delight
> Your doubts resolved you boast, your labours crowned,
> And, Eureka! your God, forsooth, is found

> Incomprehensible and infinite:
> But is He therefore found? Vain searcher, no!
> Let your imperfect definition show
> That nothing you the weak designer know ...
> Man does with dangerous curiosity
> These unfathomed wonders try;
> With fancied rules and arbitrary laws
> Matter and motion he restrains,
> And studied lines and fictious circles draws,
> Then with imagined sovereignty
> Lord of his new hypothesis he reigns.
> He reigns! How long? Till some usurper rise!
> And he too, mighty thoughtful, mighty wise,
> Studies new lines, and other circles feigns.
> From this last toil, again, what knowledge flows?
> Just as much, perhaps, as shows
> That all his predecessors' rules
> Were empty cant, all jargon of the Schools;
> That he on the others' ruin rears his throne,
> And shows his friend's mistake, and thence confirms his own.
>
> ['An Ode on Exodus iii.14']

Perhaps he did well to pass up an academic career. He may have lived in what is glibly dubbed the Age of Reason, but, while being a thoroughly reasonable man in the sense of thoughtful, undogmatic and even-tempered, he was unimpressed by larger claims made for the potential of the human mind to grasp either scientific or religious truths:

> Forced by reflective reason, I confess
> That human science is uncertain guess.
> Alas! we grasp at clouds and beat the air,
> Vexing that spirit we intend to clear.
> Can thought beyond the bounds of matter climb?
> Or who shall tell me what is space or time?
> ['Solomon', I/739-44]
>
> As through the artist's intervening glass
> Our eye observes the distant planets pass,
> A little we discover, but allow
> That more remains unseen than art can show;
> So, whilst our mind its knowledge would improve
> (Its feeble eye intent on things above),
> High as we may we lift our reason up,
> By faith directed, and confirmed by hope;

> Yet are we able only to survey
> Dawnings of beams, and promises of day.
> Heaven's fuller effluence mocks our dazzled sight:
> Too great its swiftness, and too strong its light.
>   But soon the mediate clouds shall be dispelled,
> The Sun shall soon be face to face beheld
> In all his robes, with all his glory on,
> Seated sublime on his meridian throne.
> ['Charity: a Paraphrase on 1 Cor. Chap. XIII']

Solomon disparaged his capacity despite having satisfied himself earlier in the same canto that he had successfully proved the existence of God through the exercise of logic. Elsewhere in the poem, he veers towards a modern scepticism, being dubious about angels, and finding the notion of a Creation centered upon humanity contradicted by the immensities of space:

> But do these worlds display their beams, or guide
> Their orbs, to serve thy use, to please thy pride –
> Thyself but dust, thy stature but a span,
> A moment thy duration, foolish man?
> As well may the minutest emmet [ant] say
> That Caucasus was raised to pave his way;
> The snail, that Lebanon's extended wood
> Was destined only for his walk and food;
> The vilest cockle, gaping on the coast
> That rounds the ample seas, as well may boast
> The craggy rock projects above the sky
> That he in safety at its foot may lie,
> And the whole ocean's confluent waters swell
> Only to quench his thirst, or move and blanch his shell.
> [I/549-62]

Prior enjoyed parodying philosophical schemes. The serious grappling with questions of free will in 'Predestination' are paralleled by the cheerful reductiveness of this passage in 'Alma', describing humans as puppets moved by impersonal forces:

> '   Great kings to wars are pointed forth
> Like loaded needles to the North,
> And thou and I, by power unseen,
> Are barely [merely] passive, and sucked in
> To Henault's vaults or Celia's chamber
> As straw and paper are by amber.
> If we sit down to play or set

> (Suppose at ombre or basset),
> Let people call us cheats or fools,
> Our cards and we are equal tools.
> We sure in vain the cards condemn –
> Ourselves both cut and shuffled them;
> In vain on Fortune's aid rely –
> She only is a stander-by.
> Poor men! Poor papers! We and they
> Do some impulsive force obey,
> And are but played with – do not play.
> But Space and Matter we should blame:
> They palmed the trick that lost the game.
> [II/224-42]

So our culpability in matters of little weaknesses such as drink, sex and gambling is minimised by magnetic forces which draw us irresistibly towards such things. In a skittishly droll unpublished poem, he pretended to espouse hard-line anti-materialism:

> For instance, when you think you see a
> Fair woman, 'tis but her Idea:
> [i.e., a Platonic archetype beyond the material world]
> If you her real lips salute
> Or but their shade, will bear dispute.
> "Look there!", say you, "I see a horse".
> Lord, Sir, how idly you discourse!
> "I see a horse – I'm sure that's true!"
> I say: the devil a horse see you –
> You see a horse's image, lain
> In miniature upon your brain,
> But what you take for fourteen hand
> Is less than half a grain of sand.
> Things must be stated by their nature:
> The less can't comprehend the greater.
> Now, if your groom would ne'er be able
> To set old Crop into the stable
> Unless (pray mind) the door at least
> Was something larger than the beast,
> The fellow sure would never be
> Devoid of sense to that degree
> As to desire, much less to try,
> To thrust his nag into your eye.

[given the title 'Reality and Image' in the C.U.P. text]

QED? 'The less can't comprehend the greater' is both a physical law, and Prior's characteristic means of halting speculation when he thinks it futile to carry it any further. He was interested in Lucretius, and perhaps more drawn to theories of atomism – that creation takes place perpetually through atoms combining and separating – than he liked to admit. At the beginning of 'The Ladle' (p.16) he set the scene, albeit flippantly, with the Lucretian suggestion that the gods are indifferent spectators of our affairs.

When the Divine Will is spelt out, by the angel who reveals the future of the Israelites, Solomon is given as much cause for comfort as Job. In the same grim spirit, he confronts the possibility of personal obliteration:

> ... must I pass
> Again to nothing when this vital breath
> Ceasing consigns me o'er to rest and death?
> Must the whole man (amazing thought!) return
> To the cold marble or contracted urn?
> And never shall those particles agree
> That were in life this individual he?
> But, severed, must they join the general mass,
> Through other forms and shapes ordained to pass,
> Nor thought nor image kept of what he was?
> Does the great Word that gave him sense ordain
> That life shall never wake that sense again?
> And will no power his sinking spirits save
> From the dark caves of death and chambers of the
>   grave?
> [III/543-56]

Prior knew the orthodox answer to these questions, of course, and presumably would have affirmed his belief in it, but faith is a matter of instinct: trust the animals, they know as much that is solidly worthwhile as we do. Meanwhile, all the activity in our brains will continue regardless; it needs to be known for the disorganised Babel it is, but it makes us the interesting and interested beings we are.

LET'S TALK OF GRAVES AND WORMS AND EPITAPHS

Matthew Prior led a full life. For those who lacked his curiosity, dynamism and gusto, he composed an anti-epitaph:

> Interred beneath this marble stone
> Lie sauntering John and idle Joan.
> While rolling threescore years and one
> Did round this globe their courses run,
> If human things went ill or well,
> If changing empires rose or fell,
> The morning past, the evening came,
> And found this couple still the same.
> They walked and ate, good folks – what then?
> Why, then they walked and ate again.
> They soundly slept the night away;
> They did just nothing all the day ...
> ['An Epitaph']

It emerges that this is not exactly true; and most of us could not complain too vehemently if an unsympathetic stranger were to dismiss our lives in similar terms. It was not so much the lack of incident or ambition or intelligence which Prior found offensive, but the emotional nullity and the restriction of charity to unfelt, empty social conformism:

> They gave the poor the remnant meat
> Just when it grew not fit to eat.
>   They paid the church and parish rate,
> And took, but read not, the receipt;
> For which they claimed their Sunday's due
> Of slumbering in an upper pew ...
>   Nor good, nor bad, nor fools, nor wise,
> They would not learn, nor could advise;
> Without love, hatred, joy or fear,
> They led – a kind of – as it were:
> Nor wished, nor cared, nor laughed, nor cried;
> And so they lived, and so they died.

And Prior himself? He was well aware of the transience of fame both for statesmen and poets, but he also knew his own worth, and appreciated the worth of an artistic memorial. He had been designing monuments in his head for decades, so he was not going to miss the opportunity of a very personal one just

because it might seem self-indulgent: 'For this last piece of
human vanity I Will that the sum of five hundred pounds be set
aside.' This monument was duly erected in Westminster Abbey,
with an inscription in Latin by Robert Freind (see p.52), which
lists his political offices first, but allows greater space thereafter
to his literary skills and his sense of fun, which is no doubt as it
should be. Prior's own epitaph for himself is an informal one, and
written when he might reasonably have looked forward to
enjoying more time on earth than he was actually given,
although he imagined some melodramatic finales which he was
spared:

FOR MY OWN MONUMENT

I

As doctors give physic by way of prevention,
Matt, alive and in health, of his tombstone took care;
For delays are unsafe, and his pious intention
May haply be never fulfilled by his heir.

II

Then take Matt's word for it, the sculptor is paid;
That the figure is fine, pray believe your own eye;
Yet credit but lightly what more may be said,
For we flatter ourselves, and teach marble to lie.

III

Yet, counting as far as to fifty his years,
His virtues and vices were as other men's are;
High hopes he conceived, and he smothered great fears,
In a life parti-coloured – half pleasure, half care.

IV

Nor to business a drudge, nor to faction a slave,
He strove to make interest and freedom agree;
In public employments industrious and grave,
And alone with his friends, Lord, how merry was he!

V

Now in equipage stately, now humbly on foot:
Both fortunes he tried, but to neither would trust;

And, whirled in the round as the wheel turned about,
He found riches had wings, and knew man was but dust.

VI

This verse, little polished though mighty sincere,
Sets neither his titles nor merit to view;
It says that his relics collected lie here,
And no mortal yet knows if this may be true.

VII

Fierce robbers there are that infest the highway,
So Matt may be killed, and his bones never found;
False witness at Court, and fierce tempests at sea,
So Matt may yet chance to be hanged or be drowned.

VIII

If his bones lie in earth, roll in sea, fly in air,
To Fate we must yield, and the thing is the same;
And if, passing, thou giv'st him a smile or a tear,
He cares not – yet, prithee, be kind to his fame.

INDEX OF TITLES

Works quoted in their entirety appear in bold characters

Advice to the Painter, upon the Defeat of the Rebels..............27
A Fable ('In Aesop's Tales...') 23-4
A Letter to Monsieur Boileau Despreaux 5,23
A Letter to the Honourable Lady, Miss Margaret..........50-1
Alma 9-10,14,15,45,51-2,58-9,72,76-7
An English Padlock...42
An Epistle, Desiring the Queen's Picture 21
An Epistle to Fleetwood Shephard ('When crowding folk...')......3
An Epistle to Fleetwood Shephard ('As once a twelvemonth...')
....8-9,59,71
An Epitaph..79
An Essay upon Learning 4-5,14
An Essay upon Opinion 14-5,24,27
An Ode ('While blooming youth and gay delight...') 45-7
An Ode on Exodus iii.14 57,74-5
An Ode to a Lady...29-31
An Ode...to the Queen 4
A Satire upon the Poets..4
'Besides, dear Dick, tho' you and I' 73
'Blest be the Princes who have fought' 7
Carmen Seculare...5,7,21
Charity: a Paraphrase on 1 Cor. Chap. XIII 75-6
Charles and Clenard (Dialogues of the Dead)......................5-6
Chaste Florimel...32-3
Daphne and Apollo...56-8
Down-Hall, a Ballad 61-9
Fatal Love...35
For my own Monument 80-1
Fragments Written at Down-Hall ('For when your Judge...') 25
Hans Carvel 40
Henry and Emma...47-8
'I learn to think no precept strange' 73
'Jinny the Just'..53-6
On the Coronation 26
'Phillis, since we have both been kind'..............................44
Predestination 74
'Reality and Image'..77
'Since we your husband daily see'..................................41
Solomon 6-7,8,11,24-5,57-8,70,75,76,78
The Female Phaeton 38-9
The Hind and the Panther Transversed 10

The Incurable	45
The Insatiable Priest	73
The Ladle	16-20
The Lady's Looking-glass	31-2
The New Year's Gift to Phyllis	43
The Secretary	28
The Thief and Cordelier	71-2
The Turtle and Sparrow	48-50
The Viceroy	22
To a Young Gentleman in Love	33-5
To the Honourable Charles Montague	12-3
'Who e'er a serious view will take'	25-6
Written at Paris 1700, in the Beginning of Robe's Geography	60-1
Written in the Beginning of Mezeray's History of France	13

Hugh Parry is a freelance tutor and lecturer. He has taught literature courses for ARCA residential colleges, and offered courses and day schools for Departments of Continuing Education at several universities. He was for many years involved with the W.E.A., particularly in West Yorkshire. He has taught subjects ranging from sermons to ghost stories, and authors from Euripides to R.S. Thomas. In recent years, his most cherished aim has been to blow the dust off neglected books and introduce people to the treasury of forgotten writers. Q: What is 'minor'? A: Sometimes an unfair slur – even if true, often the contemptuous shrug that dismisses a source of great potential pleasure.

As well as offering courses, Hugh Parry produces a small, mildly eccentric magazine of short articles on a miscellany of literary topics for the general reader, called 'The Wool-gatherer', as well as regular newsletters. Annual subscriptions currently are:
£10 for two 'Wool-gatherers', three newsletters, and one extra item, usually a selection from the works of a writer whom he is attempting to resuscitate.
£2.50 for three newsletters.
For overseas rates, please apply.

Hugh Parry's contact details, together with samples of his publications, can be found on his website:
www.woolgathererinwales.co.uk

This is one of a series of booklets to be published as part of The Campaign for Real Poetry (CARP). Currently available are:
The Poems of Austin Dobson
The Poems of Roger Frith
The Poetry of Mary Leapor
The Poetry of Matthew Prior

Printed in Great Britain
by Amazon.co.uk, Ltd.,
Marston Gate.